A Beginner's Guide to Studying the Bible

Augsburg Beginner's Guides introduce readers to key subjects in the past and present of the Christian tradition. Beginner's Guides strive to be readable and yet reliable, simply written but not simplistic in their approach. Each book in the series includes the information that is needed for an overview of the subject and as a solid foundation for further study.

A Beginner's Guide to Reading the Bible
by Craig R. Koester

A Beginner's Guide to the Books of the Bible
by Diane L. Jacobson and Robert Kysar

A Beginner's Guide to Studying the Bible
by Rolf E. Aaseng

A Beginner's Guide to

STUDYING THE BIBLE

Rolf E. Aaseng

Augsburg ▪ Minneapolis

A BEGINNER'S GUIDE TO STUDYING THE BIBLE

Cover design and illustration: Catherine Reishus McLaughlin

Library of Congress Cataloging-in-Publication Data

Aaseng, Rolf E.
A beginner's guide to studying the Bible / Rolf E. Aaseng.
p. cm.
Includes bibliographical references.
ISBN 0-8066-2571-6 (alk. paper)
1. Bible—Study. I. Title.
BS600.2.A27 1991
220.07'—dc20 91-28517
CIP

The paper used in this publication meets the minimum requirements of American National Standard for Information Sciences—Permanence of Paper for Printed Library Materials, ANSI Z329.48-1984.

Manufactured in the U.S.A. AF 9-2571

95 94 93 92 91 1 2 3 4 5 6 7 8 9 10

Contents

Publisher's Preface

How does someone begin to study the Bible? In this book, Rolf Aaseng shows where to start and what to do. He presents a basic, clear, and effective method of study that helps the Bible come alive for beginners.

A Beginner's Guide to Studying the Bible leads readers through a series of practical steps, illustrated by numerous examples from the Bible. The method of study presented here can be used in full or by choosing some of the suggestions. Either alternative will lead to a feeling of satisfaction as individual readers or study groups find new and deeper meaning in the Bible.

1

The Need for Study Helps

The Bible is a book for everyone. When Martin Luther began his efforts to reform the church in the sixteenth century, he based his arguments on the Bible and insisted that all Christians should know what it said. The Reformation that followed made the Bible available to lay people and established the principle that anyone who can read can grasp God's message of salvation. No special training in theology or other disciplines is necessary. A person does not have to wait for the church to give an official interpretation in order to get the meaning of a passage from the Bible.

Why then do we need a book on how to study the Bible? Because people who do not understand the nature and purpose of the Bible may not learn all they could from their reading, or they may come to wrong conclusions about its message. Furthermore, many people have never really learned to study. They survived their school experience only by remembering the required amount of information long enough to pass exams. So they may approach the Bible as they would a work of light fiction, reading to enjoy the story and feeling amply rewarded if they come across occasional statements that comfort, enlighten, or inspire them.

Such reading can be beneficial. But when we apply some basic principles of interpretation, we can find deeper meanings often not apparent on a first reading—meanings that can greatly enrich our spiritual journey.

A Different World

To get the greatest benefit from reading the Bible, we need to recognize that the world in which it was written differs greatly from the world in which we live. Most of the people of the Bible were farmers or at least part of an agricultural society, but it was much different from a modern farming community. They raised all their own food, made their own clothes, and built their own shelters. Their source of power was their own muscle, or the muscle of their animals. Their own feet and the feet of their donkeys or other beasts provided their transportation.

In their economy, based largely on barter, there were rich people, but even the wealthiest among them would be amazed at the luxuries and conveniences most of us take for granted today. In early Bible times those who could write had to laboriously imprint letters on a clay tablet. Later writers inscribed words in ink on papyrus or skins. Books were rare and individually hand written. People knew little of the geography of the world or of the existence of the solar system. The cause of illness was a mystery.

Slavery was accepted. Women had few rights and little public influence. Traditions that would seem strange to us governed society—traditions concerning marriage, family life, education, law, and commerce.

When we read the Bible or any other book, we naturally interpret what it says in the light of our own experience. But because the world of the Bible radically differs from ours, people may get many false impressions. When we read, for example, about the last supper Jesus had with his disciples before his death, we may picture them seated at a richly furnished banquet table rather than lying prone on low couches barely above the floor, as was the custom of that day.

We nod with understanding when the Bible condemns the tax collectors of Jesus' day. We may not realize that the complaint at that time was not the occasional bumbling of bureaucrats nor inequalities in the law. What bothered the people—besides their resentment at having to pay taxes to a foreign government—was the way the system operated. The tax collectors, who were despised as quislings, were required to send a specified amount to

Caesar. But Rome looked the other way when the tax collectors browbeat the people into giving much more, and that surplus went into the tax collectors' own pockets.

The Bible is written in languages foreign to us, primarily Hebrew and Greek. We have good translations, but even the best cannot perfectly reproduce the meaning and significance of the original tongue. This is particularly true of the Old Testament's Hebrew, which differs significantly from the languages of western Europe.

People in less developed countries of the world may be able to understand some of the living conditions in the Bible, but most of us struggle to comprehend what it was like.

Much of the greatness of the Bible is its ability to convey its life-giving message to readers of any generation in spite of the tremendous changes that have taken place. We should not minimize its timelessness. But the vast cultural differences between our age and the age of the Bible call for special efforts if we are to fully understand what is written.

A Unique Book

Reading the Bible also requires careful interpretation because the Bible is a unique book. It includes history, but it is not just a history book. It contains good literature, but that is not its primary feature. The Bible is the record of how God relates to his human creations. It intends to lead people to trust him. If we don't recognize its purpose, we may profit from reading it, but we will likely miss its central message.

Another reason for calling attention to principles of interpretation is that some people tend to treat the Bible as a magical book. It is doubtful that any Jews or Christians suppose that the Bible was brought down to us from heaven, as a few religions believe about their sacred books. Some may insist that God dictated every word in the Bible, but many other people, believing that it is God's Word and has power to transform lives, treat the Bible as though it has magical powers.

Some, for instance, look for God's message to them by opening the Bible at random and letting their finger fall on a particular verse. Because the Bible is filled with many wise and true statements, this method often provides help. But it can just as easily mislead.

For example, suppose your finger fell on Luke 12:18: "Then he said, 'I will do this: I will pull down my barns and build larger ones, and there I will store all my grain and my goods.' " As you try to verify this counsel, your finger lands on Luke 10:37b: "Go and do likewise." This method would give exactly the opposite message from the intent of the text.

What crimes might be committed by someone who believed that 1 Samuel 15:3 was his or her watchword for the day? ("Now go and attack Amalek, and utterly destroy all that they have; do not spare them, but kill both man and woman, child and infant, ox and sheep, camel and donkey.")

People often read the Bible without understanding its message as well as they could. The remedy is not to depend on church-appointed experts to provide the correct interpretation. History has shown that official interpreters can be wrong. Rather, readers of the Bible need to become more capable students so that they can more fully understand God's message themselves.

Of course, knowing proper study skills will not invariably lead us to the proper interpretation. Competent interpreters often disagree about the meaning of passages. Because of our human failings, no one can ever claim to have the one correct understanding of all Bible teachings.

We can still read with confidence, however. For the central message of the Bible is clear to anyone who takes the trouble to read it. We can trust the Holy Spirit to guide us to the truth as Jesus promised (John 16:13). The more skillful students we become, the more truth God will reveal to us.

> Blind unbelief is sure to err,
> And scan his work in vain;
> God is his own interpreter,
> And he will make it plain.
>
> (William Cowper, "God Moves in a Mysterious Way")

2

Before You Begin to Read

Select Your Tools

After you have decided to study the Bible seriously, one of the first questions is, which Bible? Producing new versions of the Bible has become a growth industry in America. The average person can hardly be expected to evaluate the strengths and weaknesses of the dozen or more English translations now in print. (For more information on the many English versions of the Bible, see *A Beginner's Guide to Reading the Bible,* listed on p. 99.)

The easy answer is, use any version. For it is true that God can speak to us through any of the available Bible translations. But the message may get through more easily in some than others.

Even the appearance can make a difference. It takes extra effort and motivation to study a text printed in tiny type on a crowded page. So although you may already have a Bible, if its format does not invite you to read it, buy a new one. The investment will pay dividends. Spend enough to get a copy with good-sized print, a durable binding, and (if possible) margins adequate for making notes.

You may own a copy of the King James Version, perhaps a gift from Sunday school or confirmation. (This is sometimes called the Authorized Version although the one who authorized it in 1611 was the king of England, not the church!) You may want to keep the copy for sentimental reasons, but if you intend to study the Bible seriously, you will want to get a more modern version. The King James Bible is revered as a classic literary work, but its language is archaic; we don't use thees and thous in our conversation anymore. Many of its words have different meanings today. For example, we may wonder what Jesus meant when he said, "Suffer the little children to come unto me" (Mark 10:14 KJV). Newer translations make it clear: "Let the little children come to me." To study the King James Version you almost need to translate it first.

Furthermore, since that Bible was printed, hundreds of ancient manuscripts have been discovered that are older than those available in 1611. In many places the older manuscripts have a slightly different wording from the ones used as the basis for the King James Bible. These differences don't affect any important Christian teaching, but they do enable scholars to produce a version of the Bible that is closer to the original writings. The changes help us better understand many passages.

So for your study, get a good edition of a modern translation. But which one?

Translators go about their work in two slightly different ways. Some try to produce a word-for-word translation, giving corresponding English words for the original Hebrew or Greek terms, following the same word order as much as possible. This could result in an awkward or stilted style, but most translators try to make the final result more polished. Two examples are the Revised Standard Version and the New Revised Standard Version, which both try to retain some of the style and wording of the King James Version. Other translations that follow this principle, without attempting to follow the King James, are the New English Bible and the Jerusalem Bible.

The other way to translate is to give the modern equivalent of the original words. The translator tries to convey the thoughts of the ancient writer as they would be expressed today. Thus different words, sentence structure, and style may be used. One of the most popular of such translations is Today's English Version.

An even freer translation is a paraphrase, best exemplified by the work of J. B. Phillips.

Some translations are best suited for public reading or for giving a clearer understanding. Others are better for study. Examine several versions and choose one that you can understand and memorize easily. If you are studying in a group, you may want to agree on a version that all will have. Yet often it is helpful to compare different translations. You can study with profit in any of the versions; the important thing is to get started!

Diligent Bible students will also want to use other resources in their study. The most useful are listed below. (For a more detailed description, see Appendix B, page 91.)

Concordance. Suppose you would like to know what the Bible says about prayer, or perhaps in studying a passage you come across a reference to heaven and are curious about what else the Bible says on this topic. A concordance can help you. It lists in alphabetical order all the occurrences of a word in the Bible such as *prayer* or *heaven*. Complete or exhaustive concordances are available for several versions, but abridged editions are probably more practical for the beginning student. Many Bibles contain good simplified concordances. A Bible with a center or side column of references to other Bible passages is a similar convenient tool.

Bible dictionary. Like any dictionary a Bible dictionary defines words, but it is limited to terms that occur in the Bible. In addition to a substantial definition, it usually gives much information about the word's significance and how it is used. If the term has more than one meaning, the Bible dictionary also points this out. For example, it may tell us that the word *ark* not only refers to the crude ship in which Noah survived the flood but also to a special box containing the tables of the law. It was placed in the Israelite tabernacles and temple. In some translations the word *ark* also refers to the basket in which the baby Moses was placed. A Bible dictionary also gives information about various people and places mentioned in the Bible.

English dictionary. Bible students should always have an English-language dictionary at hand. Often we do not distinguish slight differences between similar words, such as cursing and swearing, or we think of only one meaning for a word that may have several. An accurate definition sometimes helps us understand a passage better.

Commentary. A commentary offers explanations of the meaning or significance of a Bible passage. It can be especially helpful when something we read doesn't seem to make sense. For example, why did Jesus tell those he healed of leprosy to show themselves to the priest? (Mark 1:44). Or what does he mean by telling us to take up the cross? (Matt. 10:38).

Commentaries are often available in a congregational or public library. Some students may want to own one. For most, a one-volume commentary on the whole Bible is suitable. (See "For Further Reading," p. 97.)

Bible atlas. Bible reading becomes more interesting to many people if they can locate on a map the places they read about. In addition to maps of Bible lands at various periods of history, atlases give information on the life and customs of biblical times.

When you study, always have a pen or pencil, a set of colored pencils, or a highlighting marker handy so you can underline or make notes in your Bible for future reference.

Put Away Your Preconceptions

Most people who are interested in studying the Bible believe that in some way God speaks to us through this book. It is important that we allow him to speak to us directly, that we do not filter his message through a screen of ideas that we picked up from other sources.

All of us have some knowledge of what the Bible says. Even if we have never read a single verse, we have many notions about the contents of this book. We may have heard sermons in church or on the radio or TV. Perhaps we have attended Sunday school. We have read newspaper or magazine articles that refer to the Bible. We have seen artwork, listened to music, attended plays, and heard political speeches inspired by the Bible. Without realizing it, we have accumulated a number of assumptions about the Bible and what it says. Some of these assumptions are correct; many are not.

For example, most people assume that in the Christmas story there were three wise men although the Bible gives no number. It simply says they gave Jesus three kinds of gifts. The tradition that they were kings has no basis in the Bible either. The word used to describe them suggests that they were astrologers.

When we read about angels, we probably picture someone with wings—probably a chubby infant—flying through the air. The Bible rarely describes angels, but when it does, it calls them men—no hint of feathers.

The woman who came to Jesus' tomb on Easter morning "saw a young man, dressed in a white robe" (Mark 16:5). When an angel visited Gideon, the angel "came and sat under the oak at Ophrah" (Judges 6:11). Gideon chatted with him and offered food. Then the angel vanished.

Wings are associated with other heavenly creatures such as cherubim (Exod. 25:20), who don't resemble humans and seem to have a different function than angels. The word *angel* simply means messenger.

If we want to receive God's message through the Bible, it is important to clear our minds as much as possible of all preconceptions about what it says. Read the Bible as though you were coming to it for the first time. If you try to do this, you will be surprised time and again at what God will tell you. And if you can somehow imagine yourself living in the first century, you will discover even more of the Bible's treasures.

Of course, it is impossible to empty our minds completely of our life experiences. So it is necessary to call on God to help us. Before reading anything, talk to God about your intentions, your desire to learn. Prayer is a necessary first step in profitable Bible reading. Ask God to help you get rid of all previous notions so you can be open to the Bible's truths. Ask the Holy Spirit to guide you in your reading, to enable you to understand what you read and properly apply it to your life. The Holy Spirit is our teacher, our guide to truth. We need the Spirit's enlightenment to gain from our Bible study what God intends.

When you study any piece of literature, it is helpful to begin by taking a look at the entire work. What is its nature? What does it aim to accomplish? How far does it intend to take you? What is its scope? What are its limitations?

This is the way to begin Bible study too. Even if you are studying a single passage, it is good to keep in mind the purpose and nature of the entire Bible, as well as that of the individual book you are reading. The Bible is not one book; it is a collection of sixty-six books written by dozens of authors over a period of several centuries. They reflect vastly different cultural settings and even different religious understandings. These books were written for various reasons and contain many types of literature.

But they all have a similar aim: to lead people to faith in God or to encourage that faith. If you approach the Bible with a desire to learn more about this God and his intentions for you, you will be rewarded beyond your expectations.

3

How to Study a Chapter or Passage, Part 1

Whenever you study the Bible, whether alone or in a group, always begin with prayer. Ask God to send the Holy Spirit to teach you, and expect this to happen as Jesus has promised. Rely on the Spirit to give you the understanding you need when you come across a difficult passage. Pray also that God will help you use in your life what you learn.

Bible study often focuses on a single chapter or a few paragraphs within a book. This is likely to be the case in a Bible-study class or group session, where time is limited. If you are studying the Bible individually as a part of your regular devotions or quiet time, you will probably also limit yourself to a chapter or less at a time. Chapters 3 and 4 of this book give suggestions for studying short portions of Scripture. Additional helps for an extended study of an entire book are included in chapter 5.

Bible study can be described as a process of asking questions. The more questions you ask, the better you will understand the message you are intended to receive. Ask all the questions you can think of, of every element of the text. In this chapter and the next, we shall look at the kinds of questions that can be helpful as we follow these steps:

1. Make preliminary observations.
2. Note the context.
3. Discover the basic facts.

4. Examine each verse.
5. Investigate other Bible passages.
6. Draw conclusions.
7. Make use of what you have learned.

Make Preliminary Observations

Read the entire passage to discover what it seems to be about. As you do so, look for these factors:

- the kind of literature it is
- the mood
- important events, people, or places
- repeated words or ideas

KIND OF LITERATURE

Your perception of the kind of literature you are reading will affect your interpretation of the passage.

For example, when you are reading the parable of Lazarus and the rich man (Luke 16:19-31), your perception of whether Jesus was just telling a story to teach something about this life or was realistically describing heaven will affect what you learn from that parable. Your understanding of the Revelation of John will vary depending on whether you understand the book as a symbolic treatise to encourage people who are being persecuted or as a historical account of events that have taken place or as a prediction of things to come.

The Bible contains several kinds of writing. Many of them overlap; nevertheless it is helpful to identify them.

Narrative. A narrative is a story or a running account of events. In the Bible, stories are usually historical, although parables and other kinds of writing can also be narrative. Some examples include the stories of Moses, David, Ruth, Esther, Jesus, and the early Christians.

Letters. The New Testament epistles (such as Romans or 1 Peter) are letters. Some are very personal. Many were written to answer questions or to deal with specific problems. A few are general explanations of the faith.

Poetry. Poetry is found in many parts of the Bible, including the book of Psalms. Biblical poetry often uses symbolic or figurative expressions and deals with feelings and emotions more than events. It does not use rhyme but may use repeated phrases and ideas presented in a rhythmic pattern. In many versions, poetry is printed in an indented format.

Drama. The book of Job is an example. Readers can easily visualize the characters on stage as this drama of suffering unfolds.

Biography or autobiography. The book of Nehemiah is largely autobiographical as it relates Nehemiah's part in the rebuilding of Jerusalem.

Instructional material. Much of the book of Proverbs seems intended for teaching. Also, much in the prophetic books, the Gospels, and the epistles gives direction on how best to live our lives.

Official or semiofficial records. This may be a list of laws or a record of events, agreements, or accomplishments. Many examples can be found in Leviticus.

Sermon or speech. Jesus' words in Matthew 5–7 (called the Sermon on the Mount) and large sections of Deuteronomy are examples.

Apocalypse. This type of literature is not common today. It is a symbolic story telling how God will break into history to overcome present powerful evils. The book of Revelation is sometimes called the Apocalypse. Chapters 7–12 in Daniel are another example of this type of writing.

If you can identify the type of writing a passage contains, you will have some idea of what to expect. Remember that a given passage in the Bible may include more than one kind of literature.

Suppose you are going to study Philippians 2:1-11. First read the entire passage to discover what it is about. Notice the kind of writing it is. Is it a story? Obviously not. It is from one of Paul's letters, but in addition to being a letter, what other types of writing can you identify?

> If then there is any encouragement in Christ, any consolation from love, any sharing in the Spirit, any compassion and sympathy, make my joy complete: be of the same mind, having the same love, being in full accord and of one mind. Do nothing from selfish ambition or conceit, but in humility regard others as better than yourselves. Let each of you look not to your own interests, but to the interests of others. Let the same mind be in you that was in Christ Jesus.

Who, though he was in the form of God,
did not regard equality with God
as something to be exploited,
but emptied himself.
taking the form of a slave,
being born in human likeness.
And being found in human form,
he humbled himself
and became obedient to the point of death—
even death on a cross.
Therefore God also highly exalted him
and gave him the name
that is above every name,
so that at the name of Jesus
every knee should bend,
in heaven and on earth and under the earth,
and every tongue should confess
that Jesus Christ is Lord,
to the glory of God the Father.
(Phil. 2:1-11)

This short passage includes several literary forms including instructional material and poetry (the words of praise at the end may be an early hymn).

The literary form of a given passage may affect your interpretation. If it is poetry, for example, some of it may not be intended to be taken literally, as an exact description of an event. For instance, look at Isaiah 55:12:

For you shall go out in joy,
and be led back in peace;
the mountains and the hills before you
shall burst into song,
and all the trees of the field shall clap their hands.

Of course Isaiah does not expect trees to applaud; it is a metaphor, a picturesque way to speak of joy. The Psalms include many such figurative expressions. See Psalm 89:13; 102:6; 114:3-4.

THE MOOD

Observe also the style or mood. Is it hopeful, joyful, angry, matter of fact, argumentative, enthusiastic, downhearted? You may find other terms to characterize it. The passage we looked at earlier from Philippians is certainly upbeat. When you have made some observations about the mood, try to discover the reason for the attitude you found there.

IMPORTANT EVENTS, PEOPLE, OR PLACES

Skim the passage and notice what it is about. In a narrative, what people are identified or named? What is happening? Where? In epistles and other writings, learn as much about the situation as you can from the context and other resource books. Chapter 4, pages 40-41, gives additional help in getting more deeply into the passage by asking the six questions journalists use: who, what, when, where, why, and how.

REPEATED WORDS OR IDEAS

As you skim a passage, notice what is emphasized. Watch for repeated words and ideas. Authors tend to repeat the points they consider important. Noticing repetition can alert you to the main themes of the passage.

Jot down any reactions or observations you have as you read the text. You may find it useful to describe the content of the passage in general terms. After reading Philippians 2:1-11, you might write: "The author pleads for unity and humility, giving the example of Christ. He then uses beautiful poetry to praise Christ."

Note the Context

"Everything spoken or written stands in some observable relation to something else." Dr. Howard Tillman Kuist, noted Bible teacher from Biblical and Princeton Seminaries, used to require participants in his Bible classes to memorize that statement before they began their study. It summarizes the key element in his approach, and has opened the door for many people to a greater understanding of the Bible. To more fully determine the meaning of a passage, it is important to identify relationships between thoughts within the text or between this text and other passages.

One of the most significant relationships is context. This refers to the setting or surroundings of the passage—not only in the text itself but also the situation in which it was written. Never try to interpret a passage without examining what comes before and after it. Ask yourself, Why did the author insert these sentences at this point? How do they fit into the message of the book? What do they contribute to the story or argument or teaching?

If you look at a single passage without considering its context, you may completely misunderstand its meaning. Failure to consider context has led to many strange and mistaken notions.

For example, a soldier once justified his carousing to me by arguing that the Bible says, "Let us eat and drink, for tomorrow we die." He had correctly quoted 1 Corinthians 15:32, but the context makes it clear that Paul deplores this attitude.

> If the dead are not raised,
> "Let us eat and drink,
> for tomorrow we die."
> Do not be deceived:
> "Bad company ruins good morals."
> Come to a sober and right mind, and
> sin no more; for some people have no
> knowledge of God. (1 Cor. 15:32-34)

Four kinds of context can affect the meaning of the words we read—their relationships to: the preceding verses, the verses following, the entire book, and the contemporary situation.

RELATIONSHIP TO PRECEDING VERSES

The first and usually most important type of context is the relationship of the passage to the verses that come before it. Do not be influenced by chapter divisions. They do not necessarily indicate a logical dividing point. Often the preceding verses are a key to understanding the passage. They may be related in various ways, sometimes called literary constructions: (See chapter 4 for further discussion of these.)

Cause or result. These are two of the most significant relationships. Sometimes the passage gives the cause or reason for something that has just been said, or it may describe results that follow from an earlier statement. If either is the case, the passage cannot be fully understood without considering its relation to the preceding passage.

For example, Romans 5:1 says, "Therefore, since we are justified by faith, we have peace with God through our Lord Jesus Christ." But we need to read Romans 4:13-25 to see the importance of faith, and Paul gives the example of Abraham here.

Reason or explanation. Reason or explanation is another important and common relationship. The person speaking or writing explains the meaning of a previous statement, tells why he said it, or gives arguments to support it. You need to know what is being explained in order to understand the passage you are studying.

In Luke 8:11-15 Jesus clarifies the meaning of the parable of the seed and the sower told in verses 4-8. Without this explanation, the parable, with its many metaphors, may be hard to understand. Jesus said,

> "Now the parable is this: The seed is the word of God. The ones on the path are those who have heard; then the devil comes and takes away the word from their hearts, so that they may not believe and be saved. The ones on the rock are those who, when they hear the word, receive it with joy. But these have no root; they believe only for a while and in a time of testing fall away. As for what fell among the thorns, these are the ones who hear; but as they go on their way, they are choked by the cares and riches and pleasures of life, and their fruit does not mature. But as for that in the good soil, these are the ones who, when they hear the word, hold it fast in an honest and good heart, and bear fruit with patient endurance."

For another example read James 2:14-26. What arguments does James give for his assertions in the paragraph just before these verses?

Application. This is a practical relationship. The author shows how an earlier statement or conclusion applies in a specific situation, demonstrating the truth or value of what he has said or suggesting appropriate action. This may be done in several ways.

The passage may be a specific application of a general statement. In 2 Corinthians 9:6 Paul states a primary principle. Then he goes on to apply it to his readers.

> The point is this: the one who sows sparingly will also reap sparingly, and the one who sows bountifully will also reap bountifully. Each of you must give as you have made up your mind, not reluctantly or under compulsion, for God loves a cheerful giver. And God is able to provide you with every blessing in abundance, so that by always having enough of everything, you may share abundantly in every good work. As it is written,
>
> "He scatters abroad, he gives to the poor;
> his righteousness endures forever."
>
> He who supplies seed to the sower and bread for food will supply and multiply your seed for sowing and increase the harvest of your righteousness. You will be enriched in every way for your great generosity, which will produce thanksgiving to God through us; for the rendering of this ministry not only supplies the needs of the saints but also overflows with many thanksgivings to God. (2 Cor. 9:6-12)

Another type of application could be a bit of advice or an exhortation on the basis of what has just been said. For example, in Ephesians 4:24 Paul tells us to clothe ourselves "with the new self." How does this following paragraph apply that idea to our actions and attitudes?

> So then, putting away falsehood, let all of us speak the truth to our neighbors, for we are members of one another. Be angry but do not sin; do not let the sun go down on your anger, and do not make room for the devil. Thieves must give up stealing; rather let them labor and work honestly with their own hands, so as to have something to share with the needy. Let no evil talk come out of your mouths, but only what is useful for building up, as there is need, so that your words may give grace to those who hear. And do not grieve the Holy Spirit of God, with which you were marked with a seal for the day of redemption. Put away from you all bitterness and wrath and anger and wrangling and slander,

together with all malice, and be kind to one another, tenderhearted, forgiving one another, as God in Christ has forgiven you. (Eph. 4:25-32)

The application may also be a warning based on a previous statement. In Deuteronomy 12:28, after several paragraphs of instructions regarding worship practices, Moses warns the Israelites to faithfully obey these commands so God can bless them. He says, "Be careful to obey all these words that I command you today, so that it may go well with you and with your children after you forever, because you will be doing what is good and right in the sight of the Lord your God."

The author may pose questions that will lead readers to make the application themselves. The prophet Micah asked a series of questions (Micah 6:6-8) to help people understand what is most important in our relationship to God.

With what shall I come before the Lord,
  and bow myself before God on high?
Shall I come before him with burnt offerings,
  with calves a year old?
Will the Lord be pleased with thousands of rams,
  with ten thousands of rivers of oil?
Shall I give my firstborn for my transgression,
  the fruit of my body for the sin of my soul?"
He has told you, O mortal, what is good;
  and what does the Lord require of you
but to do justice, and to love kindness,
  and to walk humbly with your God?

Repetition. When an author repeats himself, we should pay particular attention. It is a signal that he is dealing with something especially important. The writer may repeat the same words, or he may restate the idea in different terms. Repetition is done for two reasons: to make something more clear, or to give emphasis.

In 1 John 4:7-12 the apostle John repeats the command to love, explaining that our love is based on God's love.

Beloved, let us love one another, because love is from God; everyone who loves is born of God and knows God. Whoever does not love does not know God, for God is love. God's

> love was revealed among us in this way: God sent his only Son into the world so that we might live through him. In this is love, not that we loved God but that he loved us and sent his Son to be the atoning sacrifice for our sins. Beloved, since God loved us so much, we also ought to love one another. No one has ever seen God; if we love one another, God lives in us, and his love is perfected in us.

In Psalm 103 the writer repeats the exhortation, *Bless the Lord*, several times to emphasize the importance of remembering God with thankfulness and praise.

> Bless the LORD, O my soul,
> and all that is within me,
> bless his holy name.
> Bless the LORD, O my soul,
> and do not forget all his benefits. . . .
> Bless the LORD, O you his angels,
> you mighty ones who do his bidding,
> obedient to his spoken word.
> Bless the LORD, all his hosts,
> his ministers that do his will.
> Bless the LORD, all his works,
> in all places of his dominion.
> Bless the LORD, O my soul.
> (Psalm 103:1-2, 20-22)

Conclusion or summary. This is similar to repetition. The passage at hand completes or brings to an end a matter the author has been discussing. Sometimes a summary of what has been said earlier at greater length can clarify the meaning of preceding verses.

For example, in Acts 2:43-47, after going into great detail about the happenings at Pentecost, the day the Holy Spirit came so powerfully on the believers of that time, the author summarizes in general terms other activities of the early Christians.

> Awe came upon everyone, because many wonders and signs were being done by the apostles. All who believed were together and had all things in common; they would sell their possessions and goods and distribute the proceeds to all, as

> any had need. Day by day, as they spent much time together in the temple, they broke bread at home and ate their food with glad and generous hearts, praising God and having the goodwill of all the people. And day by day the Lord added to their number those who were being saved.

Contrast or comparison. The author may use a contrast, that is, he may say something that presents the opposite side of his previous statements in order to make the meaning more clear. On the other hand, the passage may give an illustration, example, or comparison to make the point easier to understand.

In the last verses of Psalm 1, the author contrasts the character and fate of the wicked with the blessings that come to those who love God.

> The wicked are not so,
> but are like chaff that the wind drives away.
> Therefore the wicked will not stand in the judgment,
> nor sinners in the congregation of the righteous;
> for the Lord watches over the way of the righteous,
> but the way of the wicked will perish.
> (Psalm 1:4-6)

Refer to 1 Timothy 6:11-16 and note how Paul uses a contrast with the previous paragraph (vv. 3-10) to encourage his readers in Christian living.

In Romans 11:17-24 Paul, to help his Gentile readers understand how God has included them among his people Israel, compares them to a branch from a wild olive tree that has been grafted into a cultivated one.

> But if some of the branches were broken off, and you, a wild olive shoot, were grafted into their place to share the rich root of the olive tree, do not boast over the branches. If you do boast, remember that it is not you that supports the root, but the root that supports you. . . . And even those of Israel, if they do not persist in unbelief, will be grafted in, for God has the power to graft them in again. For if you have been cut from what is by nature a wild olive tree and grafted, contrary to nature, into a cultivated olive tree, how much

> more will these natural branches be grafted back into their own olive tree.

Continuation. The most common contextual relationship, though not the most significant, is continuation. Here the author is simply continuing a story already begun. This relationship is especially common in the Gospels, the book of Acts, and the historical books of the Old Testament. In other kinds of books an argument or instruction may be continued. When you think this relationship is present, go back to find out the background and why the story is being told.

Luke 4:38-39 tells what happened after the incident the apostle Luke has just related in verses 31-37. Look it up to see the continuity with the verses printed below.

> After leaving the synagogue he entered Simon's house. Now Simon's mother-in-law was suffering from a high fever, and they asked him about her. Then he stood over her and rebuked the fever, and it left her. Immediately she got up and began to serve them.

No connection. Sometimes there is no connection; the passage begins an entirely new topic. In 1 Corinthians 8:1-13, for example, Paul begins discussing a new problem which he has not mentioned before (although it is one of a series of problems in the congregation to which he is writing): "Now concerning food sacrificed to idols. . . ."

And of course, because nothing precedes the first paragraph of a book, the passage usually stands as an introduction and is related to what follows.

RELATIONSHIP TO FOLLOWING VERSES

Although it is not usually as important to your understanding, noting the second kind of context, the way the passage under study relates to verses that follow, can also prove valuable. This is especially true if the passage contributes to or leads up to what comes next or if the verses that follow change the meaning of the passage.

The passage under study could be related to the verses which follow it in any of the ways mentioned above. The most important relationships to look for in these verses are result and application.

Result. In John 6 it is the unbelief of many followers that results in Jesus leaving Judea and going to Galilee, as stated in the next passage:

> . . . many of his disciples turned back and no longer went about with him. So Jesus asked the twelve, "Do you also wish to go away?" Simon Peter answered him, "Lord, to whom can we go? You have the words of eternal life. We have come to believe and know that you are the Holy One of God." Jesus answered them, "Did I not choose you, the twelve? Yet one of you is a devil." He was speaking of Judas son of Simon Iscariot, for he, though one of the twelve, was going to betray him.
>
> *After this* Jesus went about in Galilee. He did not wish to go about in Judea because the Jews were looking for an opportunity to kill him. (John 6:66—7:1, italics added)

Application. After Jesus said that we should love the Lord with all our heart, soul, strength, and mind, and our neighbor as ourselves, he applied that general truth with a powerful example. Notice the last sentence in this passage:

> But wanting to justify himself, [a lawyer] asked Jesus, "And who is my neighbor?" Jesus replied, "A man was going down from Jerusalem to Jericho, and fell into the hands of robbers, who stripped him, beat him, and went away, leaving him half dead. Now by chance a priest was going down that road; and when he saw him, he passed by on the other side. So likewise a Levite, when he came to the place and saw him, passed by on the other side. But a Samaritan while traveling came near him; and when he saw him, he was moved with pity. He went to him and bandaged his wounds, having poured oil and wine on them. Then he put him on his own animal, brought him to an inn, and took care of him. The next day he took out two denarii, gave them to the innkeeper, and said, 'Take care of him; and when I come back, I will repay you whatever more you spend.' Which of these three, do you think, was a neighbor to the man who fell into the hands of the robbers?" He said, "The one who showed him mercy." Jesus said to him, "Go and do likewise." (Luke 10:29-37)

Again, in some cases there may be no obvious connection, especially when the passage being studied marks the conclusion of the discussion of a topic. But being alert to cause-and-effect relationships can often yield valuable insights.

RELATIONSHIP TO ENTIRE BOOK

The third kind of context involves the relationship of the passage to the message, purpose, or structure of the book as a whole. Earlier, we asked, Why did the author or editor insert these verses *at this point?* Now we ask, Why did he use this passage *at all* in view of his purpose for writing the book?

In order to deal with this question, we need to have some idea of the book's purpose. That is why it is good to spend time examining the entire book before you begin to dig into a single passage. (For suggestions see chapter 5.) If you have been able to discover one or more purposes of the author, you can then try to see how the passage being studied carries out the author's intention.

The passage may be related to the author's purpose in several ways. It may introduce themes, develop the story or arguments, clarify the topic, provide a climax or turning point, summarize the arguments, or even bring up a side issue.

Theme. The passage you are studying may introduce the main theme or one of the subthemes of the book. This is often the case in the first paragraph or two of a book.

In Galatians 1:1-10 the apostle Paul introduces the principal concern of the epistle—false teachers are trying to lure the Galatians away from the true gospel which Paul had preached.

> Paul an apostle—sent neither by human commission nor from human authorities, but through Jesus Christ and God the Father, who raised him from the dead—and all the members of God's family who are with me,
>
> To the churches of Galatia:
>
> Grace to you and peace from God our Father and the Lord Jesus Christ, who gave himself for our sins to set us free from the present evil age, according to the will of our God and Father, to whom be the glory forever and ever. Amen.
>
> I am astonished that you are so quickly deserting the one who called you in the grace of Christ and are turning to a

> different gospel—not that there is another gospel, but there are some who are confusing you and want to pervert the gospel of Christ. But even if we or an angel from heaven should proclaim to you a gospel contrary to what we proclaimed to you, let that one be accursed! As we have said before, so now I repeat, if anyone proclaims to you a gospel contrary to what you received, let that one be accursed!
>
> Am I now seeking human approval, or God's approval? Or am I trying to please people? If I were still pleasing people, I would not be a servant of Christ.

Note how the authors introduce their topics in the opening verses of some of the prophetic books, such as Jeremiah, Hosea, or Amos.

Development. The passage you are studying may be one of several elements in the continuing development of the story or argument presented in the book.

For example, Joshua 8:1-2 tells about the conquest of a city called Ai. This conquest was one of a series of military victories that gave the Israelites confidence as they moved into the Promised Land with God's direction.

> Then the Lord said to Joshua, "Do not fear or be dismayed; take all the fighting men with you, and go up now to Ai. See, I have handed over to you the king of Ai with his people, his city, and his land. You shall do to Ai and its king as you did to Jericho and its king; only its spoil and its livestock you may take as booty for yourselves. Set an ambush against the city, behind it."

Clarification. The passage you are studying may be an expansion of the main argument, clarifying it, suggesting implications, or emphasizing some aspect of the topic.

For example, John 6:35-40 adds ideas to a principal theme of the Gospel, that Jesus is the source of life and has been sent by the Father to give life to his people.

> Jesus said to them, "I am the bread of life. Whoever comes to me will never be hungry, and whoever believes in me will never be thirsty. But I said to you that you have seen me and yet do not believe. Everything that the Father gives me

> will come to me, and anyone who comes to me I will never drive away; for I have come down from heaven, not to do my own will, but the will of him who sent me. And this is the will of him who sent me, that I should lose nothing of all that he has given me, but raise it up on the last day. This is indeed the will of my Father, that all who see the Son and believe in him may have eternal life; and I will raise them up on the last day."

Climax or turning point. The passage in question may be a key element of the author's purpose and therefore significant to the whole book.

The turning point in the book of Exodus is 12:29-32 and the following paragraphs. After the tenth and final plague that God sent upon the Egyptians for not releasing the Children of Israel, Pharaoh commanded the Israelites to leave his country, and they began their journey to the land God had promised them.

> At midnight the Lord struck down all the firstborn in the land of Egypt, from the firstborn of Pharaoh who sat on his throne to the firstborn of the prisoner who was in the dungeon, and all the firstborn of the livestock. Pharaoh arose in the night, he and all his officials and all the Egyptians; and there was a loud cry in Egypt, for there was not a house without someone dead. Then he summoned Moses and Aaron in the night, and said, "Rise up, go away from my people, both you and the Israelites! Go, worship the Lord, as you said. Take your flocks and your herds, as you said, and be gone. And bring a blessing on me too!"

Summary of the arguments. Often this comes near the end of a book. After his lengthy comments on the futility of life, the writer of Ecclesiastes gives a final word of advice in Ecclesiastes 12:13-14. "The end of the matter; all has been heard. Fear God, and keep his commandments; for that is the whole duty of everyone. For God will bring every deed into judgment, including every secret thing, whether good or evil."

Do you agree with the author that the only important thing in life is to fear God? What do you think the word *fear* means?

Side issue. Occasionally a passage may bring up an issue not directly related to the main purpose of the book.

For example, 1 Corinthians 16:5-9 addresses Paul's travel plans, which have no bearing on the problems discussed in the letter.

> I will visit you after passing through Macedonia—for I intend to pass through Macedonia—and perhaps I will stay with you or even spend the winter, so that you may send me on my way, wherever I go. I do not want to see you now just in passing, for I hope to spend some time with you, if the Lord permits. But I will stay in Ephesus until Pentecost, for a wide door for effective work has opened to me, and there are many adversaries.

RELATIONSHIP TO THE CONTEMPORARY SITUATION

The fourth and last aspect of context deals with how the passage responds to some situation among the people of Israel or in the early church at the time it was written. We cannot always determine this from the text, but when we can identify such historical circumstances, we can better understand the significance of what is said. A commentary is often helpful in pointing out such factors. Maps can also be useful. Tracing the Israelites' journey through the Arabian desert may help us appreciate their situation.

In the following passage, the prophet Micah is responding to the greed and oppression that was prevalent among God's people in his day. He faces opposition and is being criticized for what he says.

> Alas for those who devise wickedness
> and evil deeds on their beds!
> When the morning dawns, they perform it,
> because it is in their power.
> They covet fields, and seize them;
> houses, and take them away;
> they oppress householder and house,
> people and their inheritance. . . .
> "Do not preach"—thus they preach—
> "one should not preach of such things;
> disgrace will not overtake us."
>
> (Micah 2:1-2, 6)

The passage may explain such situations, offer encouragement, or sound a warning in the light of what is happening.

John 21:20-23 may be intended to correct misunderstandings about what Jesus said would happen to certain apostles.

> Peter turned and saw the disciple whom Jesus loved following them; he was the one who had reclined next to Jesus at the supper and had said, "Lord, who is it that is going to betray you?" When Peter saw him, he said to Jesus, "Lord, what about him?" Jesus said to him, "If it is my will that he remain until I come, what is that to you? Follow me!" So the rumor spread in the community that this disciple would not die. Yet Jesus did not say to him that he would not die, but, "If it is my will that he remain until I come, what is that to you?"

For another example, look at 1 Thessalonians 4:13-18. What concern of the Thessalonian Christians do you think Paul addresses here?

> But we do not want you to be uninformed, brothers and sisters, about those who have died, so that you may not grieve as others do who have no hope. For since we believe that Jesus died and rose again, even so, through Jesus, God will bring with him those who have died. For this we declare to you by the word of the Lord, that we who are alive, who are left until the coming of the Lord, will by no means precede those who have died. For the Lord himself, with a cry of command, with the archangel's call and with the sound of God's trumpet, will descend from heaven, and the dead in Christ will rise first. Then we who are alive, who are left, will be caught up in the clouds together with them to meet the Lord in the air; and so we will be with the Lord forever. Therefore encourage one another with these words.

Although we have taken a good deal of space to explain context, it is not necessary to spend much time on this aspect of your study. Don't feel you must try to find all of the relationships mentioned. Only a few—often just one—of the points listed above will apply to any given text. Although you need not spend much time on context, do not overlook its significance.

Ask yourself, How is this passage related
- to what comes before it?
- to what comes after it?
- to the rest of the book?
- to the life situation of the first readers?

Then you will be ready to analyze the contents.

4

How to Study a Chapter or Passage, Part 2

After you have taken a look at the context so that you have some notion of why the author included this passage and placed it at this point in the book, you are ready to begin your detailed study of the text. Your task now can be summarized in two questions: Why does it say? and What does it mean?

These two questions can be answered separately, but we can often answer them both at the same time. Sometimes the answers to these questions appear so obvious that it may seem unnecessary to bother with them. But it is surprising how often we fail to observe what a sentence or paragraph actually says. This usually happens because we have some preconceived idea of what it ought to say. But at times we just fail to notice some things.

For example, we often see pictures of the wise men worshiping the baby Jesus, who is lying in a manger. But the Bible says they found him in a house, not a stable (Matt. 2:11). The fact that Herod decided to do away with all babies up to the age of two—after questioning the wise men about when the birth took place—suggests that Jesus must have been at least several months old by this time.

Discover the Basic Facts

Careful observation of what the passage actually says can minimize problems that arise because the situation then was so different from our situation now. Try to put yourself in the shoes of the writer, the first readers, or the people in the narrative. Use your imagination to re-create the scene so you feel you are actually there, experiencing the event, sympathizing with the people involved, and reacting with their feelings.

One way to do this is to ask questions as though you were a newspaper reporter. Journalists are trained to ask six questions: who, what, when, where, why, and how. Asking these questions of a passage you are studying will give you an overview of its contents. Take a look at this story from Exodus and answer the questions that follow it, which may also be applied to any passage of Scripture.

> Then Pharaoh commanded all his people, "Every boy that is born to the Hebrews you shall throw into the Nile, but you shall let every girl live."
>
> Now a man from the house of Levi went and married a Levite woman. The woman conceived and bore a son; and when she saw that he was a fine baby, she hid him three months. When she could hide him no longer she got a papyrus basket for him, and plastered it with bitumen and pitch; she put the child in it and placed it among the reeds on the bank of the river. His sister stood at a distance, to see what would happen to him.
>
> The daughter of Pharaoh came down to bathe at the river, while her attendants walked beside the river. She saw the basket among the reeds and sent her maid to bring it. When she opened it, she saw the child. He was crying, and she took pity on him, "This must be one of the Hebrews' children," she said. Then his sister said to Pharaoh's daughter, "Shall I go and get you a nurse from the Hebrew women to nurse the child for you?" Pharaoh's daughter said to her, "Yes." So the girl went and called the child's mother. Pharaoh's daughter said to her, "Take this child and nurse it for me, and I will give you your wages." So the woman took the child and nursed it. When the child grew up, she brought him to Pharaoh's daughter, and she took him as her son. She named him Moses, "because," she said, "I drew him out of the water." (Exodus 1:22—2:10)

Who. Who are the main characters? What other persons are mentioned? What are their relationships?

When. Can the incident be dated, at least in relation to other events in biblical history? Does it come before or after some other significant event? Is it the cause or result of another happening? At what point does this take place in the history of Israel or in the ministry of Jesus or Paul?

Where. Where did the incident take place? Is this significant?

What. What is the passage about? What happened? What was the situation or the problem? Is it a comment by the author or compiler? What meaning would it have had in its own day? What significance can you see in it for us today?

Why. Why is this passage included in this book of the Bible? Why is it important for me or for our church and world today?

How. How did the incident or statement come about? In what way or with what attitude or intention is the story or commentary expressed?

To find answers to some of these questions, you may need to refer to the types of resource books mentioned in chapter 2 and listed in "For Further Reading" in the back of this book. Some of the journalists' six questions fit some Bible passages better than others. They are particularly appropriate for narratives, and can be used to whatever extent they are helpful with epistles, poetry, and other kinds of literature.

Examine Each Verse

Two fundamental procedures can give you more insights into the meaning of a passage. For a thorough study of every verse or sentence, define terms and look for literary constructions or relationships.

DEFINE TERMS

Answering the question, What does it say? means basically to pay attention to every word in the text to determine its meaning. We will not understand a passage correctly if we do not know the meaning of the words used. That is obvious. Most literate persons might assume they can skip this step except when they come to a term that is unfamiliar.

But even if the words are well known, it is worth taking time to be sure of their meaning in a particular context. The author may use a word in an unusual way, or its combination with other words may give it a new significance. Examples include "Lamb of God" (John 1:29) or "the Word became flesh" (John 1:14). None of the words is unfamiliar, but to a person not acquainted with biblical concepts, these phrases are difficult to understand.

To define terms means both to identify the ones that are important and to look up key words and concepts.

Identify important words. Certain words are more important to the meaning of the passage than others. If we can identify them we can more quickly get to the heart of the passage. How?

Start by noticing words that are repeated. By using the same word or phrase more than once, the author alerts us to something he considers important.

For example, Genesis 17 repeats the word *covenant* many times, calling our attention to the importance of this term, which is significant throughout the Old Testament.

> "And I will make my covenant between me and you, and will make you exceedingly numerous." Then Abram fell on his face; and God said to him, "As for me, this is my covenant with you: You shall be the ancestor of a multitude of nations. . . . I will establish my covenant between me and you; and your offspring after you throughout their generations, for an everlasting covenant, to be God to you and to your offspring after you. . . ."
>
> God said to Abraham, "As for you, you shall keep my covenant, you and your offspring after you throughout their generations." (Gen. 17:2-4, 7, 9)

Certain words are key to the central message of the passage. Ask yourself, What word or phrase is most necessary to get the meaning? What word, if it were left out, would leave the passage meaningless or change its impact?

In John 3:3 Jesus introduces an unexpected expression, *born from above*, which becomes the center of the discussion. "Jesus answered him, 'Very truly, I tell you, no one can see the kingdom of God without being born from above.' " Try another example. What is the key expression in Mark 13:32-37?

As you grow in your faith, you will recognize words that are of special significance to Christians. Look for such words in your passage. They include: grace, love, sin, forgiveness, life, and faith.

Psalm 130 contains several such words: forgiveness, hope, love, and redeem.

> If you, O LORD, should mark iniquities,
> Lord, who could stand?
> But there is forgiveness with you,
> so that you may be revered.
> I wait for the LORD, my soul waits,
> and in his word I hope;
> my soul waits for the Lord
> more than those who watch for the morning,
> more than those who watch for the morning,
> O Israel, hope in the LORD!
> For with the LORD there is steadfast love,
> and with him is great power to redeem.
> It is he who will redeem Israel
> from all its iniquities.
> (Ps. 130:3-8)

You may find it helpful to underline or highlight important words in your Bible. In many Bible passages, the most important words are the verbs, the words that describe action or tell what someone does or what happens. Ask yourself what the verbs in your passage tell you. Do they say anything about God? Do they give you some instruction? Do they tell of something that happened in the past, is going on now, or will take place in the future?

The verbs that describe God's action in Ephesians 1 emphasize the greatness of what God has done for us (in other words, the gospel, the good news). The use of past tense makes it clear that God has already acted in all these ways.

Underline the verbs that tell what God has done.

> Blessed be the God and Father of our Lord Jesus Christ, who has blessed us in Christ with every spiritual blessing in the heavenly places, just as he chose us in Christ before the foundation of the world to be holy and blameless before him

in love. He destined us for adoption as his children through Jesus Christ, according to the good pleasure of his will, to the praise of his glorious grace that he freely bestowed on us in the Beloved. In him we have redemption through his blood, the forgiveness of our trespasses, according to the riches of his grace that he lavished on us. With all wisdom and insight he has made known to us the mystery of his will, according to his good pleasure that he set forth in Christ, as a plan for the fullness of time, to gather up all things in him, things in heaven and things on earth. (Eph. 1:3-10)

Of course, you should define any word you don't understand, whether it seems important to the meaning or not. Every Bible student should have an English dictionary nearby at all times.

Look up some words. Even if you are familiar with the important words you have identified, it is a good idea to look them up in a dictionary. As we pointed out earlier, the King James Version uses many words that have a different meaning now than when they were first written. Of course this may not be a problem in modern translations, but words often have several meanings.

Determine the meaning of the words in your passage. If a word has more than one definition, decide which one fits your passage.

For example, the word *vanity* usually refers to pride in oneself. But it also can mean empty or useless. Which is the correct meaning in Ecclesiastes 1:2?

Vanity of vanities, says the Teacher,
vanity of vanities! All is vanity.

We find another example of varied meanings in 1 Thessalonians 5. The word *spirit* is used in verses 19 and 23. In the first instance it refers to God's Spirit: "Do not quench the Spirit." In the second it is speaking of a human being's spirit: "May the God of peace himself sanctify you entirely; and may your spirit and soul and body be kept sound and blameless at the coming of our Lord Jesus Christ."

The Bible sometimes uses words in a different sense than we use them in ordinary conversation. A Bible dictionary can help us determine the biblical meaning.

The word *offering* in the Bible is not simply placing money in a plate that is passed to us during a church service. It is a literal lifting up of an animal or produce, often burning or slaughtering it. (See Leviticus 1.)

The *lawyers* whom Jesus criticized (Luke 11:45-46) were specialists in the law of Moses, not professionals who argued cases in a court of law.

Amen is not just the closing of a prayer but a strong declaration of the truth of something, as we see in the following passage:

> "Blessed be the Lord, the God of Israel,
> from everlasting to everlasting."
> Then all the people said "Amen!" and praised the Lord.
> (1 Chron. 16:36)

Sometimes the word may have a single clear meaning, but the way in which it is used may give it another meaning.

Paul uses the term *paschal lamb* in 1 Corinthians 5:7. The term refers to the lamb that was sacrificed and eaten by Jews in their observance of the Passover. In this passage, however, it is a metaphor referring to Christ, who was sacrificed for us. Readers need to know the original meaning in order to understand Paul's point.

LOOK FOR LITERARY CONSTRUCTIONS OR RELATIONSHIPS

Analyzing the literary construction or relationships will help to answer the question, What does it mean? Authors have several ways of making their meaning clear by the way they put words or phrases together in different relationships. Learn to recognize some of these ways and look for them in your passage. They will help you grasp the meaning more fully.

We shall explore some of the more common relationships or constructions. The first five were introduced in chapter 3 in the section, "Note the Context," and are presented again here with new examples and connecting words to watch for (*but, for, because, therefore*, and others).

- Comparison or illustration
- Contrast
- Reason or explanation
- Cause or result
- Repetition
- Purpose

- Means
- Questions
- Emphatic statements

This may seem like a long list, but don't let that discourage you. Begin by looking in the passages you study for one or two of the most common. After you are able to recognize them easily, try to find others. You will never find all of these types in a single passage, but if you learn to recognize them when they occur, they will help guide you to the meaning of the passage. After a time you may identify other important relationships.

Comparison or illustration. In a comparison one thing is said to be like something else with which we are more familiar. When you find a comparison ask, What is being compared? What does the comparison teach us?

Often a comparison involves only a couple of words.

In Psalm 59:16-17 David compares God to a fortress: a refuge or protection from enemies.

> But I will sing of your might;
> I will sing aloud of your steadfast love in the morning.
> For you have been a fortress for me
> and a refuge in the day of my distress.
> O my strength, I will sing praises to you,
> for you, O God, are my fortress,
> the God who shows me steadfast love.

Other times the comparison gives a fairly complete picture. Jesus often used comparisons (we call them parables) in his teaching. He said, "The kingdom of heaven is like . . .," then he compared it to something familiar to his listeners.

Comparisons are often introduced by the words *like* or *as*. In Matthew 13 Jesus uses a whole series of comparisons to explain what the kingdom of God is like. What do you learn about God's kingdom from the ones given below?

> He put before them another parable: "The kingdom of heaven is like a mustard seed that someone took and sowed in his field; it is the smallest of all the seeds, but when it has grown it is the greatest of shrubs and becomes a tree,

> so that the birds of the air come and make nests in its branches."
> He told them another parable: "The kingdom of heaven is like yeast that a woman took and mixed in with three measures of flour until all of it was leavened." (Matt. 13:31-33)

> "The kingdom of heaven is like treasure hidden in a field, which someone found and hid; then in his joy he goes and sells all that he has and buys that field.
> "Again, the kingdom of heaven is like a merchant in search of fine pearls; on finding one pearl of great value, he went and sold all that he had and bought it.
> "Again, the kingdom of heaven is like a net that was thrown into the sea and caught fish of every kind; when it was full, they drew it ashore, sat down, and put the good into baskets but threw out the bad." (Matt. 13:44-48)

Contrast. This is the opposite of a comparison. One thing is said to be different from another, frequently the exact opposite. Contrasts are often introduced by the word *but*. Ask yourself, What two things are being contrasted? What does the contrast emphasize?

For example, in Psalm 73 the writer contrasts human weakness with God's strength.

> My flesh and my heart may fail,
> but God is the strength of my heart and my portion forever. (Psalm 73:26)

Reason or explanation. The writer explains the meaning of a previous statement or gives reasons for making the statement. Explanations are often introduced by the word *for*.

Note what is being explained or supported. Consider how helpful the explanation is. Often the writer will quote another Bible passage to back up what he is saying.

In the following passage, notice how John explains the Samaritan woman's surprise that Jesus asked her for a drink.

> A Samaritan woman came to draw water, and Jesus said to her, "Give me a drink." (His disciples had gone to the city

> to buy food.) The Samaritan woman said to him, "How is it that you, a Jew, ask a drink of me, a woman of Samaria?" (Jews do not share things in common with Samaritans.) (John 4:7-9)

Cause or result. This type of statement explains what caused something or what will result from it.

Causes may be introduced by the word *because*. Results are often introduced by *therefore* or *so*; or negatively by the word *lest*.

The prophet Samuel told King Saul that because Saul did not obey God, his kingdom would be given to someone else.

> Samuel said to Saul, "You have done foolishly; you have not kept the commandment of the Lord your God, which he commanded you. The Lord would have established your kingdom over Israel forever, but now your kingdom will not continue; the Lord has sought out a man after his own heart; and the Lord has appointed him to be ruler over his people, because you have not kept what the Lord commanded you." (1 Sam. 13:13-14)

Sometimes the author says a certain result will follow if the stated conditions are met. Such statements are introduced by *if* or *unless*.

The promise of forgiveness in 1 John 1:9 has been reassuring to many: "*If* we confess our sins, he who is faithful and just will forgive us our sins and cleanse us from all unrighteousness" (italics added).

Repetition. As we have noted before, the exact word or words may be repeated, or the idea may be restated in slightly different terms. Repetition identifies an important idea. It is used either to make something more clear or to give emphasis. When you find repetition, ask yourself, Why is this repeated? If it is for emphasis, what is the idea that is so important, and why? Does it make something more clear? If so, how? Is the idea developed somehow, or is a new meaning added when the term is repeated?

Jesus uses the word *worry* several times in Matthew 6, thereby giving several reasons why we don't have to be worry warts.

> "Therefore I tell you, do not worry about your life, what you will eat or what you will drink, or about your body, what

> you will wear. Is not life more than food, and the body more than clothing? Look at the birds of the air; they neither sow nor reap nor gather into barns, and yet your heavenly Father feeds them. Are you not of more value than they? And can any of you by worrying add a single hour to your span of life? And why do you worry about clothing? Consider the lilies of the field, how they grow; they neither toil nor spin, yet I tell you, even Solomon in all his glory was not clothed like one of these. But if God so clothes the grass of the field, which is alive today and tomorrow is thrown into the oven, will he not much more clothe you—you of little faith? Therefore do not worry, saying, 'What will we eat?' or 'What will we drink?' or 'What will we wear?' " (Matt. 6:25-31)

Purpose. Purpose is often introduced by the words *that, so that, in order that,* or *to*. Statements of purpose are especially significant constructions because they let us know the intended result of something. When you find a purpose statement, ask what purpose is indicated; whose purpose it is; and how it is related to the topic being discussed.

In Exodus 9:14, for example, God says that his purpose in sending the plagues that afflicted the Egyptians was that the Egyptians should acknowledge him as the only true God. "For this time I will send all my plagues upon you yourself, and upon your officials, and upon your people, so that you may know that there is no one like me in all the earth."

Switching to the New Testament, notice what God's purpose was in sending his Son to the world, according to John 3:16.

Means. The author tells how something is to be accomplished. The introductory word is often *through* or *by* or *in*.

Paul, in 1 Corinthians 12:3, says that people are able to make a confession of faith only by means of the Spirit's power. "Therefore I want you to understand that no one speaking by the Spirit of God ever says 'Let Jesus be cursed!' and no one can say 'Jesus is Lord' except by the Holy Spirit."

Questions. Questions often help an author to get his point across. They may be included as part of the account of an event: someone asks a question. In such cases ask yourself, Who posed the question? What was their purpose? How was it answered? What do we learn from the dialogue?

In Matthew 22, Jesus' opponents asked him questions to try to discredit him; he asked questions in return to expose their trickery and to teach a truth.

> Then the Pharisees went and plotted to entrap him in what he said. So they sent their disciples to him, along with the Herodians, saying, "Teacher, we know that you are sincere, and teach the way of God in accordance with truth, and show deference to no one; for you do not regard people with partiality. Tell us, then, what you think. Is it lawful to pay taxes to the emperor, or not?" But Jesus, aware of their malice, said, "Why are you putting me to the test, you hypocrites? Show me the coin used for the tax." And they brought him a denarius. Then he said to them, "Whose head is this, and whose title?" They answered, "The emperor's." Then he said to them, "Give therefore to the emperor the things that are the emperor's, and to God the things that are God's." When they heard this, they were amazed; and they left him and went away. (Matt. 22:15-22)

In other kinds of writing the author may direct a question to the readers in order to introduce a new idea or to convince readers of the truth of his argument.

The prophet Malachi uses questions to get people's attention and impress on them that they were not doing right. "Will anyone rob God? Yet you are robbing me! But you say, 'How are we robbing you?' In your tithes and offerings!" (Mal. 3:8).

Emphatic statement. In most English versions, an emphatic statement is identified by an exclamation mark. This is a sentence that indicates excitement, strong feeling, or anger. When you see such a statement, ask yourself why the author or the person quoted feels so strongly.

When Jesus discovered people selling animals in the temple, he made a whip of cords and drove the moneychangers out with these words: " 'Take these things out of here! Stop making my Father's house a marketplace!' His disciples remembered that it was written, 'Zeal for your house will consume me' " (John 2:16-17).

Before concluding your study of a passage, look again for connecting words to make sure you have not overlooked a significant construction or relationship which these words introduce.

- *As* or *like* may make comparisons.
- *But* may introduce contrasts or change.
- *For* may indicate a reason or explanation.
- *If* may state a condition.
- *Because* may indicate a cause.
- *Therefore* and *so* may introduce results.
- *That* may indicate purpose.
- *Through* or *by* may suggest means.

Investigate Other Bible Passages

Often we can gain further understanding of a text, or even of a single word, by referring to other Bible passages that deal with the same subject. Some of these passages are indicated in footnotes in many Bibles; be sure to look up all of them. Center-column reference Bibles or chain reference Bibles give a selected list of passages on similar topics. A more complete source for related references is a concordance, which lists all uses of a particular word. These are helpful tools.

Check first to see if the author deals with the same subject, even using the same terms, elsewhere in the book of the Bible you are studying. If so, does this help you to understand what he means? Does the word always mean the same thing, or are other ideas sometimes added?

Paul uses the word *mystery* six times in Ephesians. In five of the occurrences he is speaking of God's plan, that is, the gospel. If we just had the reference in 6:19, that's the only meaning we would know. "Pray also for me, so that when I speak, a message may be given to me to make known with boldness the mystery of the gospel."

But earlier statements in chapter 3, especially verse 9, help us to see the particular aspect of the gospel he is referring to: the inclusion of the Gentiles in God's kingdom.

> In former generations this mystery was not made known to humankind, as it has now been revealed to his holy apostles and prophets by the Spirit: that is, the Gentiles have become fellow heirs, members of the same body, and sharers in the promise in Christ Jesus through the gospel. (Eph. 3:5-6)

God's plan is to include all people, his whole creation, in his future, including, of course, the Gentiles.

Pay particular attention to direct quotations from other parts of the Bible. If your passage quotes a verse from the Old Testament, look it up. In many Bibles the reference is footnoted and printed at the bottom of the page.

Does its original use help you understand the meaning in the later passage? Has the passing of centuries or the development of a new situation given a better understanding of what was said earlier? Note how other passages show agreement with or differences from the idea expressed in your passage. How does another passage reinforce or add meaning to the verse you are studying? Sometimes the wording of the quotation is not exactly the same as the original. Does this help you understand it better?

Peter, in Acts 4:11, speaks of Jesus as a stone: "This Jesus is 'the stone that was rejected by you, the builders; / it has become the cornerstone.' " He is referring to a statement made in Psalm 118:22: "The stone that the builders rejected / has become the chief cornerstone." Jesus' own statement in Matthew 21:42 also makes this connection.

Scripture interprets Scripture. A good principle in Bible study is to let clear passages explain the more difficult ones. To trace a particular topic through several books of the Bible can be a fascinating adventure.

Draw Conclusions

Up to this point you have been making observations and gaining information. Now it is necessary to integrate your findings with the words of the text so you can arrive at some conclusions about the meanings they are intended to convey.

ASK INTERPRETIVE QUESTIONS

Good Bible students ask a lot of questions. Why questions are especially helpful. Why did the author give attention to this subject or tell this story? What is his objective? Why did he use this word rather than another that means almost the same thing? What do the words actually say? Are they meant to be taken literally? Why did he repeat these words or ideas? Why did he use these particular literary devices (comparison, contrast, etc.)? Why did he emphasize this idea or event so much?

What assumptions has he made? How is the teaching of these verses related to similar or contrasting teachings elsewhere in Scripture or the traditions of the church? Would this concept be understood differently by the original readers, or by people today who live in different circumstances from mine? If its message is taken seriously, what are its implications or probable results?

The more questions you can raise and answer, the more you will understand the passage. Answering the questions may be somewhat easier if you can think of yourself as being on the scene. Imagine that the writer is speaking directly to you, and that you are one of the people in the narrative or a member of the group to whom he is writing.

For example, if you are studying Joshua 24, try to imagine how Joshua felt. He was near the end of his life; the people would soon be without his leadership. He remembered the many times their faith failed. He wanted to say something that would encourage and inspire the Israelites to go forward and claim all the land God had promised them. He tried to challenge them, forcing them to make a choice, and making his own commitment publicly.

You might pretend to be someone in the crowd who is listening with admiration mingled with shame as you recall Joshua's inspired leadership and your own failures. You feel anxiety as you realize he won't be your leader much longer, and since so much remains to be done, it all depends on you and your neighbors. You are impressed by his example and are caught up in the enthusiasm of the crowd as you shout your intention to be true to God. How does that perspective affect your study of this passage?

> Then Joshua gathered all the tribes of Israel to Shechem, and summoned the elders, the heads, the judges, and the officers of Israel; and they presented themselves before God. And Joshua said to all the people, "Thus says the LORD, the God of Israel: Long ago your ancestors—Terah and his sons Abraham and Nahor—lived beyond the Euphrates and served other gods. Then I took your father Abraham from beyond the River and led him through all the land of Canaan

> and made his offspring many. I gave him Isaac; and to Isaac I gave Jacob and Esau. I gave Esau the hill country of Seir to possess, but Jacob and his children went down to Egypt. Then I sent Moses and Aaron, and I plagued Egypt with what I did in its midst; and afterwards I brought you out. When I brought your ancestors out of Egypt, you came to the sea; and the Egyptians pursued your ancestors with chariots and horsemen to the Red Sea. When they cried out to the Lord, he put darkness between you and the Egyptians, and made the sea come upon them and cover them; and your eyes saw what I did to Egypt. Afterwards you lived in the wilderness a long time. Then I brought you to the land of the Amorites, who lived on the other side of the Jordan; they fought with you, and I handed them over to you, and you took possession of their land, and I destroyed them before you. . . . I gave you a land on which you had not labored, and towns that you had not built, and you live in them; you eat the fruit of vineyards and oliveyards that you did not plant.
>
> "Now therefore revere the Lord, and serve him in sincerity and in faithfulness; put away the gods that your ancestors served beyond the River and in Egypt, and serve the Lord. Now if you are unwilling to serve the Lord, choose this day whom you will serve, whether the gods your ancestors served in the region beyond the River or the gods of the Amorites in whose land you are living; but as for me and my household, we will serve the Lord." (Joshua 24:1-8, 13-15)

APPLY YOUR DISCOVERIES TO THE TEXT

Try to integrate what you have learned into the text, taking the verses in order. Many students do this by making notes in the margin of their Bible. Others underline words or draw lines from one word to another to indicate important concepts or to show relationships. Relationships or themes can also be indicated by the use of colored pencils or markers. For example, you might use red to mark statements that add to your understanding of God's grace and blue for those that help you understand your need. A well-marked Bible is a valuable resource for Christian growth and future study.

A more complete way to retain what you have learned is to write down what the passage now says to you. To be able to write your conclusions you must clarify them in your own mind. What you write will also be of value whenever you refer to that passage again in the future. Keep your written comments in a notebook, organized according to books of the Bible.

Go back to the beginning of the passage and state briefly its context. Then proceed verse by verse or sentence by sentence (verses are not necessarily the best units for study) and comment on your understanding of the meaning and significance of the text, making use of the discoveries you have made in your study.

For an example of how this might be done, let us use Galatians 5:16-24 as our passage of study.

> Live by the Spirit, I say, and do not gratify the desires of the flesh. For what the flesh desires is opposed to the Spirit, and what the Spirit desires is opposed to the flesh; for these are opposed to each other, to prevent you from doing what you want. But if you are led by the Spirit, you are not subject to the law. Now the works of the flesh are obvious: fornication, impurity, licentiousness, idolatry, sorcery, enmities, strife, jealousy, anger, quarrels, dissensions, factions, envy, drunkenness, carousing, and things like these. I am warning you, as I warned you before; those who do such things will not inherit the kingdom of God.
>
> By contrast, the fruit of the Spirit is love, joy, peace, patience, kindness, generosity, faithfulness, gentleness, and self-control. There is no law against such things. And those who belong to Christ Jesus have crucified the flesh with its passions and desires.

This passage continues Paul's discussion of the implications of the gospel for Christian living as we accept the leadership of God's Spirit rather than trying to keep the law by ourselves. It begins by contrasting life lived under the influence of the Holy Spirit with the destructive effects of living to satisfy the desires of the flesh, that is, sinful human nature.

The terms *Spirit* and *flesh* are emphasized throughout the passage. Paul explains that the Spirit of God and human nature are opposed to each other, and he urges us to consciously follow the

Spirit's leading. Otherwise the flesh may keep us from doing what we really want to do (v. 17). We can avoid this problem if we follow the guidance of the Spirit, who frees us from the domination and condemnation of the law (v. 18).

Paul goes into detail, describing the works or behavior characteristic of the flesh. Some of them (immorality, impurity, licentiousness) involve sexual or moral misconduct (licentiousness means disregarding moral standards). Some concern indulging self to excess (drunkenness, carousing). Others involve following a false god (idolatry, sorcery). But most refer to divisive and selfish attitudes toward others (vv. 19-21). Deliberate continuation in such actions puts a person outside God's kingdom (v. 21).

In contrast, those led by God's Spirit will find it natural, without the compulsion of law, to exhibit attitudes of consideration for others (vv. 22-23). Christians are free to act in this way because their evil desires have been destroyed by Christ's death. This thought also occurs in Romans 6:1-4.

The passage is followed by an exhortation which summarizes this paragraph.

In the above example we have noted context, identified *Spirit* and *flesh* as significant words, and defined or restated several terms. We have called attention to contrasts, explanations, illustrations, and results. We have referred to another passage which says something similar.

Conclude your comments with a summary that identifies the main concerns of the text. A summary of the above passage might read as follows: Paul warns us against being guided by the selfish desires of the world, which are contrary to God's will, for this results in destructive conduct that places us under the condemnation of the law. Those who believe in Christ follow instead the guidance of the Spirit, who enables them to exhibit attitudes of love toward others.

When formulating a summary, questions such as these may help:

- What does this passage tell about God, Jesus, or the Holy Spirit?
- What does it tell about humanity or the world we live in?
- What does it teach about sin, evil, and suffering?

- What does it teach about God's purpose for his creation, his interest in us, his love for us?
- What does it teach about God's grace, salvation, forgiveness, or eternal life?
- What does it teach about our worth, our value?
- What advice is given for Christian living?
- Are there any promises? Any warnings? Any commands or instructions?

Often it is helpful to write a brief paraphrase of the passage, restating what it says in different, simpler words. An example of a paraphrase of John 1:29-34 is given below, followed by the words as they appear in the Bible.

> When John saw Jesus walking toward him he said, "Here comes God's sacrifice for our sins. I baptized him, but he is more important than I am. My job is to point him out to you. I saw something like a dove come down on him; otherwise I wouldn't have known who he was. But God had told me: 'When you see my Spirit coming down on someone you baptize, this is the one who will bring the Holy Spirit to people.' I saw it and I'm telling you that this is God's Son."

> The next day he saw Jesus coming toward him and declared, "Here is the Lamb of God who takes away the sin of the world! This is he of whom I said, 'After me comes a man who ranks ahead of me because he was before me.' I myself did not know him; but I came baptizing with water for this reason, that he might be revealed to Israel." And John testified, "I saw the Spirit descending from heaven like a dove, and it remained on him. I myself did not know him, but the one who sent me to baptize with water said to me, 'He on whom you see the Spirit descend and remain is the one who baptizes with the Holy Spirit.' And I myself have seen and have testified that this is the Son of God."

Make Use of What You Have Learned

When you have gone this far, so that you have discovered at least some answers to the questions, What does it say? and What does it mean?, you are not yet done with your study. Bible study is not an end in itself. We don't study the Bible just for the sake of engaging in study, even though it can be an interesting and enjoyable adventure. We study for a purpose. Something should happen as a result of our studying the Bible.

Therefore we now specifically ask the question: What does it mean to me? Many references have already been made about applying the biblical text to our lives, but this is a good point to pull such learnings together and ask, "Now that I have studied and made some discoveries and learned something, so what? Where do I go from here?"

Diligent Bible study will have an effect on our lives. It will result in growth, and that means change, for there is no growth without change. If we are not prepared to change in some way, we better not risk studying the Bible.

Bible study may lead to a difference in what we think or believe. It may give us a new attitude toward God, toward ourselves, toward other people, toward the church, toward the world. It may spur us to change the ways we spend our time and money, and the kind of activities we engage in.

Bible study can affect our hearts as we learn more about God's great love for us. We feel freer and less burdened, knowing we are forgiven and loved. That reassurance expands our ability to love, and we may feel a renewed sense of purpose in our lives. We joyfully join in with the songs and prayers of thankfulness and praise expressed by psalmists and other biblical writers.

To apply our study to ourselves we can ask questions like these:

- What have I learned that I didn't know before?
- What misunderstanding has this study cleared up for me?
- What have I learned about God that I did not know or had forgotten? How will this affect my relationship with him?
- What have I learned about myself?
- What have I learned about God's plan for me? How should I use this knowledge?
- What promises have I found that will encourage my faith?
- What warnings apply to me?
- What advice or instruction fits my needs?
- How will this passage influence the way I think, feel, and act today and tomorrow?

- How will it affect my relations with other people?
- How can I put my new learning into practice?
- How does what I have learned apply to problems in my life or in my community?

Write in a few sentences what you have learned, including a commitment to do something.

Finally, conclude your study by telling God in prayer what you have found, asking forgiveness for any sins that have been revealed, requesting further enlightenment in understanding God's intentions for you, asking for wisdom and courage to carry out what you now understand that God wants you to do, and thanking him for all you have learned.

5

How to Study an Entire Book

A common approach to Bible study is to deal with a single book of the Bible in its entirety, such as the Gospel of Matthew, the book of Ruth, Daniel, or Ephesians. This chapter is intended especially to help in this kind of study. You will note that some of the suggestions are similar to those proposed for studying a chapter or shorter portion, but other ideas here are particularly useful for studying a book. You may also find these guidelines helpful when studying a shorter passage as outlined in the previous chapters.

The steps described below can be used with any biblical book. You can carry out this kind of study by yourself, but it will be more rewarding for you if you do it together with others so you can share your discoveries. And again, begin with prayer as you launch your study.

We shall proceed in two stages, first laying the groundwork:

- Make general observations
- Learn about the writer
- Learn about the intended readers
- Discover the author's (or compiler's) purpose in writing
- Get the whole picture

Then we will move on to getting the message:

- Study each part
- Summarize and apply

A helpful resource for your study is *A Beginner's Guide to the Books of the Bible*, listed in "For Further Reading" at the end of this book. It gives introductions to all sixty-six books of the Bible, with a brief overview of author, date, purpose, and contents of each book. Do your own exploring first, but turn to this resource for further information.

Make General Observations

Before you begin a detailed study, skim through the entire book. Go through it as rapidly as you can, preferably more than once. Don't try to read every word or worry about understanding it. This will come later. Do this skimming at one sitting. Many books of the Bible are just a few pages long, for example, Ruth, Amos, Philippians, or 1 John. Most can be read in less than an hour. But don't take time to read every word yet. Just skim rapidly.

As you do so, write down your impressions or observations. What do you notice as you turn the pages? Not everyone will observe the same things. There are no correct answers. Write down what *you* find.

You might look for:

- the kind of literature it is
- the mood
- important events, people, or places
- repeated words or ideas

KIND OF LITERATURE

As mentioned in chapter 3, your perception of the kind of literature a book is may affect your interpretation of its message. Obviously, if you read a cookbook expecting it to be a history book, for example, you will be frustrated!

Chapter 3 described and gave examples of ten kinds of literature found in the Bible, noting that combinations of literary forms are common. Even though they often overlap, identifying them in a given book or passage will aid the reader's understanding. They are listed again here with the names of other books of the Bible that contain that kind of literature.

Narrative. Genesis, Joshua, 1 and 2 Samuel, the Gospels, Acts of the Apostles.

Letters. New Testament epistles such as Galatians, Ephesians, Philippians.

Poetry. Song of Solomon, portions of Isaiah.

Drama. Job.

Biography or autobiography. Esther, Ruth, the Gospels.

Instructional material. James and other epistles.

Exhortations and discourses. Prophets such as Hosea.

Official or semiofficial records. 1 and 2 Chronicles.

Sermon or speech. Hebrews, portions of the Gospels.

Apocalypse. Part of Daniel, the Revelation of John.

As you look at the book you are studying as a whole, what is the predominant literary form? What other forms do you find?

MOOD

The author may be writing with a particular point of view. Recognizing that can help you appreciate what you'll be reading. The writer may be objective or personally involved, clearly taking sides.

The mood can be described in many ways. For example, the book may strike you as being:

- joyful like Philippians
- gloomy like Lamentations
- formal or impersonal like Hebrews
- informal or personal like Philemon
- hopeful like 1 Peter
- critical like Amos

You may think of other terms to characterize a book you are studying.

IMPORTANT EVENTS, PEOPLE, OR PLACES

What is the book about? Many books concentrate on certain events or people. See if you can identify them. Using the questions who, what, when, where, why, and how can be helpful (pages 40–41). Here are some examples of important events, people, and places.

Exodus is primarily concerned with the event that gives the book its name: the exodus or departure of the Israelites from Egypt to Canaan. (Check Map 1 to see where this happened.)

The historical book of 2 Samuel (and much of 1 Samuel) tells the story of David the king.

Ezra is about the return of the Jews from captivity.

Acts focuses on the activities of Peter and Paul and traces the spread of Christianity from Jerusalem to other cities. (See Map 4.)

REPEATED WORDS OR IDEAS

As mentioned in chapter 3, authors tend to repeat terms or ideas that they consider important. Noticing them will alert you to the main themes of the book.

The word *life* occurs more than forty times in the Gospel According to John. This is a significant concept in his book.

In Galatians Paul talks repeatedly about law and grace. Can you find a term that is used repeatedly in Philippians?

The many repetitions of the word *Lord* in the book of Jonah reminds us that God is the important figure in the story—not the fish!

Noting important events or ideas also directs you to the primary meaning of the book.

Learn about the Writer

Some concepts in the book will be more understandable if you know something about the author and the people to whom he wrote. (As far as we know, all the biblical writers were men.) First look for any information the book itself may give you.

Does the author identify himself? If so, find out all you can about this person from the book you are studying or from other Scripture passages. Using cross-references in your Bible or a concordance, which lists all uses of a particular word (including names) in the Bible, will help you.

Romans and several other epistles claim Paul as their writer. The book of Acts and several epistles, especially Galatians, provide details of his life.

> You have heard, no doubt, of my earlier life in Judaism. I was violently persecuting the church of God and was trying to destroy it. I advanced in Judaism beyond many among

> my people of the same age, for I was far more zealous for the traditions of my ancestors. But when God, who had set me apart before I was born and called me through his grace, was pleased to reveal his Son to me, so that I might proclaim him among the Gentiles, I did not confer with any human being, nor did I go up to Jerusalem to those who were already apostles before me, but I went away at once into Arabia, and afterwards I returned to Damascus. (Gal. 1:13-17)

Does the author say anything about his circumstances? What he has experienced will influence what he writes.

John, the writer of Revelation, says he was on the island of Patmos "because of the word of God and the testimony of Jesus" (1:9). This suggests he had been exiled by authorities hostile to Christianity.

Read Ephesians 3:1 to learn Paul's situation when he wrote this letter.

Whether the author gives his name or not, we can tell something about him by the way he uses language or by his knowledge of customs, events, or details of geography.

The writer of John is well acquainted with many localities in Judea, suggesting that he is from that land and thus most likely a Jew.

The author of Matthew is familiar with Old Testament Scriptures, and frequently quotes and interprets them. Undoubtedly he was Jewish.

The writer of Acts also wrote the Gospel According to Luke. In Acts 1:1 it is referred to as "the first book." "In the first book, Theophilus, I wrote about all that Jesus did and taught from the beginning." And Luke was apparently a companion of Paul on his later travels. Notice the use of the pronoun *we* in Acts 16:11. "We set sail from Troas and took a straight course to Samothrace, the following day to Neapolis." This information fits well with the tradition that Luke was the author of Acts.

Most of the books of the Bible are anonymous, but almost all have been traditionally assigned to certain individuals. Later study has indicated that the tradition may not always be correct. Several books were probably compiled from many sources by some individual. Most commentaries will give the arguments pro and con for various theories about authorship. Whether we can be sure about the author in every case need not affect our study, however. Over the centuries, the church has concluded that the books, of whatever origin, have messages of great significance for us.

Learn about the Intended Readers

Does the writer say to whom he is writing or what their situation is? The introductory verses of most New Testament epistles give us the name of the writer and the recipients, according to the customary format for correspondence in that day.

For example, Romans is addressed "to all God's beloved in Rome" (1:7). Paul says they are saints, that is, believers, and that their faith has become known in other parts of the world. They apparently met for worship in the house of Prisca (sometimes called Priscilla) and Aquila, who are referred to in Acts 18:2 as well as here. Paul writes, "Greet Prisca and Aquila . . . Greet also the church in their house . . . Greet Andronicus and Junia, my relatives who were in prison with me" (Rom. 16:3, 5, 7). Some believers seem to have suffered imprisonment for their faith.

The book of 1 Peter refers to trials the letter's recipients had experienced, suggesting that they were undergoing or had suffered persecution. "In this you rejoice, even if now for a little while you have had to suffer various trials" (1 Peter 1:6). "Beloved, do not be surprised at the fiery ordeal that is taking place among you to test you, as though something strange were happening to you" (1 Peter 4:12).

In 1 Corinthians, Paul deals with a number of problems that members of that congregation had referred to him. They included factions and disunity in the congregation, open immorality, lawsuits among members, and questions about marriage.

> For it has been reported to me by Chloe's people that there are quarrels among you, my brothers and sisters. (1 Cor. 1:11)

> It is actually reported that there is sexual immortality among you, and of a kind that is not found even among pagans; for a man is living with his father's wife. (1 Cor. 5:1)

> When any of you has a grievance against another, do you dare to take it to court before the unrighteous, instead of taking it before the saints? (1 Cor. 6:1)

> The husband should give to his wife her conjugal rights, and likewise the wife to her husband. . . . Do not deprive one another except perhaps by agreement for a set time, to devote yourselves to prayer, and then come together again, so that Satan may not tempt you because of your lack of self-control. (1 Cor. 7:3, 5)

In the case of epistles written to congregations, it is helpful to know something about the community. This information is available in most commentaries.

To realize that Corinth had a reputation for gross immorality helps us to understand why Paul warns the Christians in the congregation there against prostitution and other immoral acts.

Often the writer doesn't identify by name the recipient of his writings, but he may hint at the kind of person (or community) that will read it.

Matthew's many references to the Old Testament suggest that Jews who knew the Scripture and regarded it as authoritative would be reading the book.

Mark translates Aramaic words such as *Talitha cum* ("Little girl, get up!" [5:41]) and explains Jewish customs, such as ceremonial washings (7:3-4), which suggests that he expected non-Jews to read his book.

Discover the Author's (or Compiler's) Purpose

Knowing why a book was written greatly helps us understand its message. Sometimes the writer clearly states a purpose. Luke says he is writing in order to assure Theophilus, and no doubt others like him, that what they had been taught about Jesus was true (Luke 1:1-4). John, in his gospel, waits until the end to state his purpose. You can find it in John 20:31.

At other times we can get some idea of the author's intention from what he includes, or from the emphasis he gives to certain subjects. We may not be able to form any conclusion about this, however, until we have studied the entire book.

Paul wrote to the Galatians to set forth clearly the true gospel, to counter false teachings being put forward by some in their midst.

After you have gained what knowledge you can from the book you are studying, you may wish to consult a commentary or other book that gives Bible background. Such books can provide a great deal of information about the historical and cultural situation. But don't read other books before you have learned all you can from the text itself. Otherwise you will deprive yourself of the thrill of making your own discoveries, and what you learn won't be as firmly imbedded in your memory.

Get the Whole Picture

Try to get some idea of the book's subject matter and scope before you begin studying individual verses or chapters.

COMPARE THE BEGINNING AND THE END

Note any differences or movement between the beginning and end of the book: in time, place, people mentioned, or subject matter. This will tell you something about what the book covers.

For example, at the beginning of Exodus the Israelites are in Egypt, suffering oppression. At the end they are in the wilderness on their way to the Promised Land, having been freed from Egyptian domination. The book then can be expected to explain how this change came about.

The first chapter of 1 Kings describes the last days of King David. The last paragraph of 2 Kings (1 Kings and 2 Kings are best studied together) informs us that a later king is a prisoner in Babylon. We can expect that the two books will explain how the strong nation established by David came to such a sorry end.

Notice where the events at the beginning of Acts take place; then compare the location of the action in the last chapter. One of the purposes of the book is to explain how and why the church shifted its center away from its starting point. (Map 2 may be helpful.)

TITLE THE CHAPTERS

On the basis of your quick skimming, write on a sheet of paper a tentative title for each chapter. What does it seem to be about?

Don't try to summarize the chapter. Pick one idea that can help you to recall the contents. Who is involved? What happens? Where does it take place? Is some thought repeated or emphasized?

Of course, since you are skimming and not yet reading every word, you may not always recognize the main thrust of the chapter. Don't worry about that. You will probably want to alter your list after you have studied the chapter, anyway. There is no right or wrong way to name chapters. Use whatever terms best help you remember its contents. Each person's outline will be different. Some may seem better than yours, but you will remember your own outline longer than someone else's.

Many Bibles print headings for chapters or paragraphs. These may be helpful to you, but try to use your own words. They will mean more to you. Some chapters include many topics; choose one that is most memorable. Be as specific as possible, using terms that apply to only one chapter. For example, rather than saying, "Jesus does a miracle," say, "Jesus raises Lazarus."

The six chapters of Ephesians might be given titles like these:

1. God chose us
2. We are united in Christ
3. Paul prays for his friends
4. How to use God's gifts
5. Rules for living
6. The whole armor of God

As you become more familiar with this process, see if you can condense your titles to one or two words.

This brief look at contents can alert you to significant features of the book. You may find that a large proportion of the chapters deals with a certain person or a particular event, or that the same theme occurs again and again. This often gives you a clue about why the book was written or put together.

For example, in the Gospel of Mark, the amount of space given to the death and resurrection of Jesus suggests the overriding importance of this part of his ministry. Or the repetition of God's promises to succeeding generations in Genesis indicates the significance of what was known as *the covenant* in Israel's history.

LOOK FOR AN OUTLINE

If you can detect some evidence of structure in the book, you can more easily follow the author's argument or narration. Your list of chapter titles may suggest natural groupings. Thus, chapters 14–17 in John's Gospel are Jesus' farewell teachings and prayer. See if you can identify the common theme that runs through Exodus 7–12.

Structure can be discovered in several other ways. Sometimes you may realize that a certain introductory or summary statement is repeated, indicating natural divisions.

The phrases *the generations of* or *the descendants of* are repeated in Genesis 2:4, 5:1, and eight other places in the first eleven chapters of Genesis. See if you can find them. The instances where this phrase occurs can provide an outline of this part of the book.

In Matthew the phrase *When Jesus had finished* is repeated in 7:28; 11:1, and three other places. Many students divide the book into sections where this sentence occurs.

Definite changes in content also give a basis for natural divisions. The book may concentrate on a certain person for a while then switch to someone else.

The first chapters of Acts primarily talk about Peter and his activities. But he is mentioned for the last time in Chapter 12 (except for a brief incident in chapter 15). After that Paul is the main character. This suggests that the book has two main parts.

The book of Judges could be divided according to the various "judges," or leaders, who play an important role in the account: Ehud, Deborah, Gideon, Jephthah, and Samson.

The book may describe events that take place in different locations or at different times in history.

Exodus 1–15 takes place in Egypt. In chapters 16–18 the Israelites are traveling. The rest of the book is centered around Mount Sinai. So the book can be divided into three sections for studying. You can trace their progress using Map 1.

The Book of Judges deals with several periods in Israel's history, perhaps separated by many years. Movement from one period to another is often indicated by summary statements which are italicized in the following passage.

> So Moab was subdued that day under the hand of Israel. *And the land had rest eighty years.*
>
> *After him* [Ehud] came Shamgar son of Anath, who killed six hundred of the Philistines with an oxgoad. He too delivered Israel.
>
> *The Israelites again did what was evil* in the sight of the Lord, after Ehud died. (Judges 3:30—4:1)

Sometimes there is a decided change in the style of writing. Most students note such a change at Isaiah 40 and believe that two or more different persons wrote the book we call Isaiah.

Often the subject matter changes. The first part of Ephesians is an exposition of the gospel message, telling how God in his grace has saved us, bringing us from death to life through Jesus Christ. In Chapter 4 the author begins a new section, explaining what effects God's saving acts are to have in the lives of Christians.

Sometimes it is possible to identify a climax or turning point in the book. This may be the high point of the story, the strongest argument, or a crucial event or statement. At times it will be marked by a doxology (a sentence praising God, perhaps sounding like a hymn or a benediction) or even by the word *Amen*.

This is especially noticeable at the end of Chapter 3 in Ephesians, which makes it clear that the first section is being concluded.

Many students find the climax of each of the Gospels at the point when Peter, speaking for the twelve, confesses his faith in Jesus as the Christ. In Mark this comes in verse 29 of chapter 8. Note how the story changes after this confession of faith. Attention now turns to the coming suffering and death of Jesus.

> He asked them, "But who do you say that I am?" Peter answered him, "You are the Messiah." And he sternly ordered them not to tell anyone about him.
>
> Then he began to teach them that the Son of Man must undergo great suffering, and be rejected by the elders, the chief priests, and the scribes, and be killed, and after three days rise again. (Mark 8:29-31)

Some books move to a climax near the end. The high point of the Book of Revelation is the announcement of final victory after a long series of conflicts and troubles. But this doesn't come until chapter 21.

Sometimes there will be no clear outline. The epistle of 1 John is an example of a book that does not seem to follow a logical outline. But if you can, try to discover how the sections of a book are related. Are certain ideas or themes connected? Is there progression, one section leading naturally to the next? Is there a suggestion of contrast?

Don't be discouraged if you can't seem to detect an outline or climax at this point. It becomes easier with practice. You will be able to see the structure more readily as you study the portions in detail.

FIND RELATED BOOKS

Does the book you are studying seem to be related in some way to another book in the Bible? If so, reading the other book may give you insights into the message of this one. Until you are well acquainted with the Bible, you may have to consult resource books such as *A Beginner's Guide to the Books of the Bible* or a commentary to learn which books are related.

For example, Kings and Chronicles cover the same period of history but from different points of view. Chronicles seems to tell the story more from the viewpoint of the Southern Kingdom of Judah and emphasizes worship.

Revelation has some similarities to parts of Daniel and Ezekiel and borrows some of its symbolism from them.

The Book of Acts seems intended to follow Luke (Acts 1:1) so that Luke and Acts can be thought of and studied as a unit.

Each of the four Gospels tells the story of Jesus from a particular point of view. We gain a deeper understanding of the Gospel if we identify the particular emphasis of each account, rather than trying to harmonize them into one story.

Study Each Part

Now you have completed the first stage, laying the groundwork, and are ready to begin the second stage of getting the message. Looking more thoroughly at the contents is, of course, the heart of your study. This is where you will spend the most time. Organize your study by chapters or by the divisions you have just discovered. Go through each paragraph, each verse. As explained earlier, you may decide to change the tentative titles you gave to the chapters. You may also wish to study a particular passage several times from different perspectives.

Use the suggestions in chapters 3 and 4 for studying a chapter or passage. You will discover that some tasks may already have been accomplished (identifying the kind of literature; noting important people, events, and places), but you can discover much more as you note more about the context and examine each verse.

Summarize and Apply

When you have gone through the whole book, review your summaries of each section or chapter (as explained in chapter 4) to see how the separate parts are related and how the order in which they appear helps the author achieve his purpose. Then the structure or outline becomes more apparent. Constructing a chart is often helpful for summarizing. (A chart for the Acts of the Apostles appears below.) Reexamine your original findings about the purpose of the book. If your ideas are not still valid, restate the purpose to reflect your new understanding.

<table>
<tr><td>Chapters</td><td colspan="2">1–12</td><td colspan="4">13–28</td></tr>
<tr><td>Main character</td><td colspan="2">Peter</td><td colspan="4">Paul</td></tr>
<tr><td>Focus</td><td colspan="2">Jews</td><td colspan="4">Gentiles</td></tr>
<tr><td></td><td>1–7</td><td>8–12</td><td colspan="4"></td></tr>
<tr><td>Church</td><td>Founded</td><td>Scattered</td><td colspan="4">Extended</td></tr>
<tr><td>Area</td><td>Jerusalem</td><td>Judea,
Samaria</td><td colspan="4">Ends of the earth</td></tr>
<tr><td>Center</td><td colspan="2">Jerusalem</td><td colspan="4">Antioch</td></tr>
<tr><td></td><td colspan="2"></td><td colspan="3">13–20</td><td>20–28</td></tr>
<tr><td></td><td colspan="2"></td><td colspan="3">Paul free</td><td>Paul
imprisoned</td></tr>
<tr><td></td><td colspan="2"></td><td colspan="3">Journeys</td><td>Caesarea/
Rome</td></tr>
<tr><td></td><td colspan="2"></td><td>1</td><td>2</td><td>3</td><td></td></tr>
</table>

Then summarize the entire book in terms of its purpose. Write out the main points of the book as you have discovered them. Indicate how or to what extent the author has achieved his purpose. Identify the key teachings that are presented. Finally, write down what you personally have learned from your study.

For example, in studying Joshua you might observe that the book moves toward a climax in the last chapter when the people of Israel reaffirm their faith in God. The preceding chapters prepare for this climax by telling how the Israelites entered the land, conquered it, and distributed it, all in accord with the promise and intention of God. You might conclude that possession of the Promised Land came about because Israel followed the instructions of God who promised this result and made it possible. This may lead to your own reaffirmation of faith and a determination to follow God in your life.

A Sample Study

As an abbreviated example of how we might carry out a book study, let's use the epistle of Galatians.

GENERAL OBSERVATIONS

- This is a letter, the style of which is argumentative and instructive.
- Paul, the writer, uses strong language; he seems to be upset.
- There is opposition to Paul's message.
- Paul gives details about his life.
- Frequently used terms include *freedom and slavery* and *law and grace*.

WRITER

The author is identified as Paul. The book of Acts gives information about his life, including his ministry among the people to whom he is writing.

THE RECIPIENTS

Christians in Galatia, probably Gentiles.

THE PURPOSE

Paul is writing to combat false teachings that threaten to undo his work.

CONTENTS

Tentative chapter titles:
1. Paul is alarmed by false teachers.
2. Paul criticizes Peter.
3. Abraham shows that faith is what counts.
4. If you try to save yourself by law you are a slave.
5. Don't lose the freedom Christ gives.
6. Exhortations for Christian living.

STRUCTURE OR OUTLINE

- Chapters 1–2: the problem
- Chapters 3–4: arguments
- Chapters 5–6: exhortation

RELATED SCRIPTURE

The book of Acts gives an account of Paul's ministry in Galatia and also tells of the arguments in the church over the matter of keeping the law. (See especially chapter 15.)

The book of Romans also deals with the problem of the function of the law and how it contrasts with grace. Like Galatians, it also uses the example of Abraham, especially in chapters 3–8, to show that faith is what counts.

SUMMARY AND APPLICATION

Paul, upset by some who teach that people must keep the law in order to be considered Christians, argues that this approach will nullify what Christ has done. He defends his credibility as a teacher of truth and argues that the law's function is to show us our need of salvation, which God gives freely on the basis of what Christ has done. He encourages his readers to resist the tendency to reimpose the law, urging them to respond to God's gift by serving others.

The book teaches me that the true gospel is the good news that God has saved me through grace. I must be aware of the human tendency to try to do something to merit salvation. I am unable to contribute anything. God has done it all! In response to God's law, I want to live my life the way God directs us to live—not in order to *be* saved but because I *have been* saved.

If you have been studying alone, find opportunities to share your learnings with others—not as though you now know something they don't, so you must teach them, but to witness what God has done for you through his Word. This will strengthen your faith in Christ and will prompt others to share with you what they have learned. You can encourage one another in a Christian response to what God has taught you and serve the Lord in the strength the Spirit gives!

6

Where to Begin

You have decided that you are going to study the Bible and you have some idea of how to go about it. But now your question may be: Where shall I begin?

Many people begin, quite naturally, at the beginning—with Genesis, the first book of the Bible. This works well for a time. Although there are a few difficult passages, the stories in Genesis about the creation of the world, about Noah, Abraham, Isaac, Jacob, and Joseph are interesting. To some of us they are familiar, which makes them easy reading.

So the new student goes ahead into Exodus. That too is an interesting story as we sympathize with the mistreated Israelites and rejoice with them as the Egyptians get their comeuppance and the people of God set off on their journey to the Promised Land.

But just as the Israelites seemed to get bogged down in the wilderness, the Bible student begins to find it heavy going too. Before getting halfway through Exodus, interest wanes with the seemingly endless rules and instructions that appear to have no meaning for today. If students push themselves to complete Exodus, the next book is even worse. Leviticus is full of minute details of rules and rituals that deal with matters quite foreign to us. At this point the beginning student may give up.

It doesn't have to end that way.

Not all parts of the Bible are equally interesting or relevant to the modern reader. Some parts are admittedly more difficult, not only to read, but to understand. If you are just beginning to study the Bible, it makes sense to start with parts that are easier and more interesting and more immediately significant. What are these parts? Where should a new student begin?

Start with the Gospels

One of the Gospels (Matthew, Mark, Luke, or John) is a good place to start because the story of Jesus is the central message of the Bible, the basis of the Christian faith.

But even here there are choices. Which of the four Gospel accounts is best to start with? Many choose Luke. He is a skillful writer and tells the story in an interesting way. The best-known parables of Jesus are in his book. Luke's Gospel would be a good starting place.

John is the favorite Gospel of many Christians, but he is more philosophical and likes to explore difficult ideas at great length. It may take a while to learn to appreciate him.

Matthew, too, has proponents, but the book is longer and includes long sections of dialogue.

That leaves Mark, which may be the best choice for a beginner. Mark is the shortest of the four Gospels. It is a book of action, repeatedly using words like *immediately* to rush the reader on his or her way. Many scholars believe it was written with the action-oriented Romans in mind, so it often appeals to busy North Americans.

After completing Mark, your appetite may be whetted to learn more about Jesus; then Luke would be a good choice. (If you began with Luke, Mark would be a good follow-up). Or you may prefer to take on something a little different, leaving the other Gospels for later.

Acts would be a good book to read next. It is another book of action, with exciting developments and crucial conflicts. It tells how the gospel message spread to the non-Jewish populations, which include most of us, and into the parts of the world where many of our ancestors came from.

Next you might choose an epistle, to see how the early church interpreted the meaning of Jesus' life and death. Philippians is probably the easiest to start with, and it has an upbeat message of encouragement.

Then it may be a good time to go back to the beginning and read the interesting stories of Genesis and the first part of Exodus. The book of Exodus is especially important because that event, the Israelites leaving the oppression they suffered in Egypt, is the key event in the Old Testament. Later writers refer to it often. Genesis is also important, for it gives the first promises of God to overcome the disastrous results of sin.

By this time, you may be ready to range more widely in the Bible. Read the other Gospels and other epistles, especially Ephesians, Colossians, and 1 Peter.

You will also want to become acquainted with the Psalms. But we approach the book of Psalms differently than most biblical books. It too can be studied analytically, and you would learn much. But the psalms (or songs) of David and other writers are not intended to be studied, but rather to express the psalmists' thoughts and feelings about God. As we read these psalms and think about them, they can help us express to God what we are feeling as well. Psalms are often used for private or corporate worship. Many congregations regularly include them in their orders of service. The Israelites sang them, and today's hymnals offer various musical settings for many of the psalms, either quoting them directly or paraphrasing them.

Rather than attempting to analyze these poetic writings, try to put yourself in the writer's frame of mind. Often you will find that he expresses your feelings in a way you find difficult to do. Note his honesty. He complains to God and even dares some mild criticism. This can encourage you to be honest in your own dealings with God. After all, God knows what you think and feel whether or not you express it out loud. And God wants us to be honest with him as he is with us. The psalms also provide good material for daily devotional reading.

Read It All

So far we have touched only a small part of the riches available in the Bible. You will want to become acquainted with all of them.

In order to accomplish this, you will want to do another kind of reading in addition to the kind of study we have outlined in this book.

This reading can be done more rapidly, without taking time for detailed study. Try to go through the whole Bible so you will be acquainted with what it contains and can identify portions you will want to come back to later for study. In this reading, you don't have to read every page. If you get into a section that seems needlessly complicated, skip a few chapters. Take another look at them later on. Make it your aim to read something from the Bible every day.

Many people use a devotional guide: a short Bible passage accompanied by some comments. These are helpful, but don't limit your daily reading to them. Many prefer to read in the morning—it gives them their marching orders for the day. Whatever plan you follow, read thoughtfully until you find a message from God to you for that day.

Following a reading schedule is often helpful. If you want to go through the Bible in one year, that goal can be accomplished by reading three chapters every day and five on Sundays.

But don't worry about quantity. It is more important to read a few verses, get their meaning, and apply it to your life than to cover several books.

Most of us need some help to remain faithful in our Bible readings. In addition to following a schedule, joining a Bible study group in your church or neighborhood can help. This not only encourages you to keep at your reading, it will also enrich your study as you gain the insights of others.

Whatever procedure you follow, get started! The first and most important rule of Bible study is: Read. God will do the rest.

7

When You Bog Down

After you have been studying the Bible for some time, you may experience a dry season. Your study seems to be harder work than before. It is not as enjoyable. You aren't getting as much out of it as you used to. What's wrong?

Don't be discouraged. What you are experiencing is not unusual, nor is it an indication that you have fallen out of God's favor. Rather it is evidence that you still are a human being, vulnerable to sin and human weakness. As long as we are on this earth, we will go through ups and downs in our spiritual journey. But how can we get back on the high road?

First of all, talk to God about it. Tell him how you feel. Admit that studying has become a chore, that you find it boring or too difficult. Express your dissatisfaction with this situation and your desire to experience again the joy of productive study. Confess your inability to accomplish this by yourself and ask for help. Recall God's past goodness and thank him in anticipation of future blessings.

Then reflect on how you are carrying on your study. Have you begun to think about quantity rather than quality, pushing yourself to cover a certain number of verses or chapters? Is your busy life putting pressure on you to get through your study as quickly as possible? Have you settled into a routine that follows the same path each time, rather than exploring new avenues in search of God's surprises?

Perhaps receiving a message from God is no longer the most important activity in life, or your approach has become stale. You have lost that sense of anticipation as you seek God's wisdom.

If you have begun to lose interest while you are reading through a confusing passage of history or a long list of names or laws, turn to another portion of Scripture. If the epistles seems to be getting repetitious, try reading a historical book. If history no longer excites, sample the prophets. If you've had enough of them, go back to the Gospels.

Some sections of the Bible provide little interest to modern readers. Don't feel guilty if you decide to jump over some chapters (even a whole book) or if you put aside a particularly difficult passage. Later on, when you have become more adept in your study skills and have grown in your understanding of God's Word, you may find these chapters of greater interest; that is the time to study them.

If you are frustrated because you cannot understand something you are studying, or if you come to a conclusion that doesn't seem right to you, spend a little more time on the passage, repeating the steps suggested in previous chapters. Try especially to find other Bible references that deal with the subject. They may be able to clarify the matter.

If the problem remains, go on to another study. In the meantime talk over your difficulty with other Christians. They may have experienced the same feeling and learned how to overcome it. Keep the problem in mind as you pray, worship, reflect on your faith, and continue to read your Bible. Trust God to help you understand what is important for you.

Do not let failure to understand something stop you from studying. As humans, none of us has complete understanding of all God's revelation. "Now we see in a mirror, dimly," Paul observed (1 Cor. 13:12), but he assures us that we shall someday understand fully. For the present, however, we have trouble grasping the meaning of some biblical statements. Even scholars who have spent their entire lives studying the Bible cannot explain everything perfectly, and they often disagree on how certain paragraphs should be interpreted.

If you have bogged down for any reason, perhaps you should try a different kind of Bible reading for a time. Rather than engaging in concentrated study, try reading simply as a devotional exercise. Make use of the psalms especially. Take time to meditate and pray on the basis of short passages. Use your hymnbook to get biblical messages in a different form.

Are you sharing your study with others? God's Word is addressed to the believing community—a group, not primarily individuals. If you have been studying alone, try to find a group to study with. Join a class in your congregation. You don't have to wait until a pastor is available to lead you. Invite your neighbors and friends to your home, where you can share your findings with one another, giving each other encouragement when things get difficult. Under the guidance of the Holy Spirit, you can help each other avoid errors that can come easily when we read or study by ourselves.

Try reading other Christian literature. God often speaks to us through the words of other believers. Commentaries and other books that interpret the Bible are helpful. But keep in mind that such books, though they may contain much of value, do not always agree with one another. The fact that something is printed in a book does not necessarily make it correct.

Whatever you do, don't give up. Most of us have plateaus in our learning when we seem to be making no progress. But if we keep at it, the plateau will become a stepping stone to a higher level. Continue your study, learn what you can, and trust God to open your mind to receive more. Gradually the Holy Spirit will help you understand more and more of God's message. You will be amazed at how much of the Bible speaks to you!

Anyone who is willing to spend the time and effort can discover what God has to say to us in the Bible. Be assured that you will be blessed by a diligent study of this book, God's Word for us. For God has promised, "My word . . . shall not return to me empty, but it shall accomplish that which I purpose, and succeed in the thing for which I sent it" (Isa. 55:11).

Appendix A

Other Methods of Study

Many methods of Bible study have been developed to meet particular situations, depending on whether one is studying individually or in a group. Group study methods depend on the number of participants and their needs and interests, the time available, and the nature of resources and facilities. This book describes one method in detail, but the principles discussed can be used in other methods.

THE VASTERAS METHOD

This method is especially useful when the members of the group have not done any preparatory study before coming together and when the leader has no special training. The name comes from its origin in Sweden.

Participants individually read the prescribed Bible passage. As they read, they make symbolic marks in the margin of their Bibles as follows:

¡ This represents a candle. Make this mark alongside any statement from which you gain a new insight.

↑ Make an arrow pointing up whenever you read something that tells you about God, especially his grace or the gospel.

↑ Make an arrow pointing down at every place the passage speaks directly to you or describes you, especially if it points out a need.

? Place a question mark where there is something you don't understand.

When the allotted time is over, let each member of the group report his or her findings. Begin by asking each one to list his or her candles—the new insights they have received. There will likely be a great variation in what the participants found helpful.

Next, report on the arrows pointing up—what each one learned about God and his dealings with us. Follow this by noting the arrows pointing down—often confessions of need or guilt, which call for reemphasizing the grace of God (arrows pointing up).

By this time, the insights shared may have answered many of the questions participants had marked. If some remain, decide on a course of action. Either agree to do further research on the topic, or ask a pastor or some other Bible student for an explanation.

Here is an example of how this method might work with the assigned passage, Philippians 4:4-7. Candles might mark these ideas: we are always to rejoice, our prayer requests should also include thanksgiving, and peace is ours in Christ.

Arrows up might mark these concepts: the Lord is always at hand, we can make our requests known to God, and God promises us peace and security in Christ.

Arrows down might indicate my confession that I don't always rejoice and let others know about my faith, I am sometimes anxious rather than prayerful, and I sometimes try to solve problems my own way rather than talking to God about my needs.

Question marks might show up when we wonder how it is possible to rejoice at all times, or what this peace that God promises is like.

DRAMATIZATION OR ROLE PLAY

Many Bible passages can be dramatized, especially if there are a number of characters involved in dialogue or action. For example, the story of Joseph and his brothers or the Last Supper lend themselves to this kind of treatment. After reading the passage aloud, let members of the group take the roles of the various characters. Let them make up their lines, retelling the Bible narrative in their own words. This could be done more than once with new characters in the various roles. This will often result in different interpretations.

The purpose of dramatization or role playing is to make the event more real to us and to help us understand the point of view of the persons involved.

For some passages you might be able to use puppets or hand motions (people stay behind a screen and carry out actions with their hands above the screen while a narrator reads the Bible story).

"YOU ARE THERE"

The purpose of this method is the same as above: to make the passage more real and to help us better understand the dynamics of the situation. This is done by imagining you are a participant or a witness to what happened in the passage under study.

Assume the role of a newspaper or TV reporter. Give your account of what transpired as you would give it to your viewers or readers. Interview the persons involved. Imagine how they would respond, or let another member of your group take the role of the person interviewed. Other members of your group might suggest other questions. If you want to do a bigger production, videotape the interviews or record them on an audiocassette.

Another variation would be to hold a press conference with the main character, portrayed by someone in your group. Let everyone else ask questions.

Write a diary entry. Imagining that you are a witness or participant in the incident described, write in your diary what you experienced and how you felt about it.

TELL THE STORY

Imagine you are telling—or actually tell—the story of this passage to a three-year-old, to an eight-year-old, or to an adult who has never heard the story before.

Write a paraphrase of the passage. See if you can convey the same message in your own style of expression. When you can retell something in your own words, you have grasped the important concepts.

COMPARING VERSIONS

Using as many different versions or translations as you can obtain, read the passage in each. Note agreements on important points. Identify differences. Consider the significance of the differences and possible reasons for them. What new insights do you gain from the various translations?

RESEARCH

Using a Bible with columns of cross-references, or a chain-reference Bible, look up the cross-references given for a particular word. What do they add to your understanding?

Identify significant words in a passage and look up these terms in a concordance. What do you learn about the meaning of the term from other verses in which it is used? What does this add to your understanding of the passage at hand?

Choose a word that is commonly used in the Bible or in church, such as *forgiveness* or *sin*. Look up all references to this word in a concordance. Now define the word as it is used in the Bible, and summarize its significance for the Christian faith.

This method could also be used with important biblical people. Learn as much as you can about an individual by looking up all biblical references to him or her. How does this give you a better understanding of the person and his or her role in God's activity?

ARTISTIC EXPRESSION

If you or members of your study group are interested in music, poetry, or art, read a passage and try to think of pieces of music, poems, or various art expressions that reflect, interpret, or relate to the message in some way. For example, the text of Handel's *Messiah* is taken verbatim from various passages in the Bible.

Using one or more artistic media, express what the passage means to you. You might compose a melody or create a painting or sculpture. You could write new words for a familiar hymn tune such as the doxology, or interpret the meaning of a passage through dance.

GREAT PASSAGES

Many passages of the Bible have come to have special meaning to many Christians. For a worthwhile Bible study, examine in detail some of the following.

- Matthew 5–7: The Sermon on the Mount
- Matthew 13: Parables of the Kingdom
- Luke 15: The Prodigal Son and other parables
- John 1: The prologue to John's gospel
- John 17: The high priestly prayer of Jesus
- Acts 10: The conversion of Cornelius
- Romans 8: More than conquerors
- 1 Corinthians 13: Paul's essay on love
- Hebrews 11: The faith chapter
- Exodus 20: The Ten Commandments
- Isaiah 53: A foretelling of Christ's suffering
- Psalms 19, 23, 51, 90

REPETITION

Read the same passage several times, looking for something different each time. For example, you might read a passage from the point of view

- of Israel or the early church
- of your congregation
- of your own needs
- of the needs of the world

Or you could read it several times, looking for a particular relationship each time, such as comparisons, statements of purpose, or cause and result.

PERSONAL OVERVIEW

In studying a book of the Bible, for each chapter write down:

- subject
- lesson learned
- favorite verse

Or for each chapter write down:

- an example to follow
- an error to avoid
- advice or exhortation to heed
- a promise to believe
- a reason to thank God
- a prayer to offer

LUTHER'S "LITTLE WREATH"

Martin Luther suggested that as we study the Bible we should construct a "wreath," a whole formed by interwoven parts, by looking for four things:

- What does it teach about God, about my neighbors, and about me?
- What reason does it give me to thank God?
- How does it help me toward salvation?
- What does it remind me to pray for?

Appendix B

How to Use Study Resources

A CONCORDANCE

A concordance lists in alphabetical order words found in the Bible, giving the chapter and verse where they are used. Complete or exhaustive concordances list all the words and all the occurrences of each word. Shorter concordances list only those likely to be of greatest interest to most people.

A concordance is indispensable when you want to look up a particular verse but cannot remember the exact wording. For example, you may recall that Jesus once said something about wearing a yoke. If you look up the word *yoke* in a concordance, you will find several references to Old Testament verses in which it is used. Usually the word in question will simply be represented by its first letter, and given in a brief context. Here are some examples.

Deut. 28:48 an iron *y.* on your neck

1 Kings 12:4 Your father made our *y.* heavy

Obviously these are not what you are looking for. You will also see some New Testament references, such as

Matt. 11:29 Take my *y.* upon you.

Recognizing this as the verse you want (or at least knowing that a statement from Jesus would be in the Gospels) you can look up the verse in your Bible and read it in its entirety.

A concordance is also helpful in studying biblical topics. Suppose you wanted to make a study of the Passover. If you looked up the word *Passover*, you would find several references including these:

Exod. 12:11 It is the *p*. of the Lord
Matt. 26:17 preparations for you to eat the *P*.
John 18:39 release someone for you at the *P*.

The Exodus passage gives the origin of the Passover. The Matthew and Luke references relate the Passover to the Last Supper of Jesus with his disciples. The verse in John shows that the Roman government took notice of the Passover. These verses would give you a start for your study of the topic.

CENTER-COLUMN REFERENCES

Some Bibles have a center (or side) column of Bible references to verses that relate to the text on that page. They are of great value in finding one or more passages that help explain the meaning or significance of terms used.

If you should be studying the account of Zechariah's encounter with the angel in the temple, you might be interested in reading about other appearances of angels. Beside the word *angel* in Luke 1:11 is a small letter *o* (see Figure 1). Find that letter in the list of references in the center column. It refers to Acts 5:19. This is another passage in which angels are mentioned. A concordance would give you a more complete listing of such passages.

A similar system is used in chain-reference Bibles. These, however, give only the next occurrence of the term in the Bible.

BIBLE DICTIONARY

Many Bible terms are foreign to us. Some of them are defined in English dictionaries. For others, or to get a fuller explanation of the word's meaning, consult a Bible dictionary.

For example, in reading the account of the conquest of Canaan by the Israelites, you may come across references to "high places," which God's people are told to destroy (see Numbers 33:52). Later on, the Israelites are criticized for building such high places themselves (see 1 Kings 14:23). What is so evil or dangerous about a high place? A Bible dictionary will explain that these were sites on top of hills where people worshiped false gods.

derly account[d] for you, most excellent[e]
Theophilus,[f] 4so that you may know
the certainty of the things you have
been taught.[g]

The Birth of John the Baptist Foretold

5In the time of Herod king of Judea[h]
there was a priest named Zechariah,
who belonged to the priestly division
of Abijah;[i] his wife Elizabeth was also
a descendant of Aaron. 6Both of them
were upright in the sight of God, ob-
serving all the Lord's commandments
and regulations blamelessly.[j] 7But
they had no children, because Elizabeth was barren; and they were both
well along in years.
8Once when Zechariah's division
was on duty and he was serving as
priest before God,[k] 9he was chosen by
lot,[l] according to the custom of the
priesthood, to go into the temple of the
Lord and burn incense.[m] 10And when
the time for the burning of incense
came, all the assembled worshipers
were praying outside.[n]
11Then an angel[o] of the Lord ap-
peared to him, standing at the right
side of the altar of incense.[p] 12When
Zechariah saw him, he was startled
and was gripped with fear.[q] 13But the
angel said to him: "Do not be afraid,[r]
Zechariah; your prayer has been heard.

2Ch 8:14
1:9 [l]Ac 1:26
[m]Ex 30:7,8;
1Ch 23:13;
2Ch 29:11;
Ps 141:2
1:10 [n]Lev 16:17
1:11 [o]S Ac 5:19
[p]Ex 30:1-10
1:12 [q]Jdg 6:22,
23; 13:22
1:13 [r]ver 30;
S Mt 14:27 [s]ver
60,63; S Mt 3:1
1:14 [t]ver 58

1:15 [u]Nu 6:3;
Lev 10:9;
Jdg 13:4; Lk 7:33
[v]ver 41,67;
Ac 2:4; 4:8,31;
6:3,5; 9:17;
11:24; Eph 5:18;
S Ac 10:44
[w]Jer 1:5;
Gal 1:15
1:17 [x]ver 76
[y]S Mt 11:14
[z]Mal 4:5,6
[a]S Mt 3:3
1:18 [b]Ge 15:8
[c]ver 34;
Ge 17:17
1:19 [d]ver 26;
Da 8:16; 9:21

Zechar
can I be su
and my w
19The an
el.[d] I stand
I have bee
tell you t
you will
speak[e] un
cause you
which wil
time."
21Meanw
ing for Ze
he stayed
22When h
speak to t
seen a visi
making si
unable to
23When
pleted, he
his wife
and for fiv
sion. 25"T
me," she
shown his
disgrace[g]

The Birth

26In the
angel Gab
Galilee, 27t
ried to a

Figure 1

The Israelites' use of high places indicated that they were forsaking the true God and worshiping idols.

Bible dictionaries provide other helpful information as well. If you, like most people, find it difficult to keep the history of the various kings of Israel and Judah straight in the books of Kings and Chronicles, a Bible dictionary can help you. Under the heading *chronology* most Bible dictionaries list in parallel columns the kings of each country according to their date in history, as well as a column listing other concurrent events in world history.

COMMENTARIES

You learn so much more in Bible study if you do the digging yourself and do not simply read what someone else has discovered in the text. But when the Bible does not provide enough information for us to fully understand the message of a particular passage, commentaries can be very helpful.

For example, in reading the Book of Ruth, you may wonder why Boaz had to negotiate with another man before he could proceed with his courtship of Ruth. A commentary can explain the customs and laws of that day pertaining to rights and requirements in transferring property, especially when it involves relatives. It will also explain the procedures that accompanied certain legal transactions, such as taking off one's shoe (see Ruth 4:7).

Most commentaries also provide good introductory articles which can be of great value in understanding the message of the Bible.

BIBLE ATLAS

Most people enjoy tracing their travels on a map. Referring to maps can also add interest to Bible study. As an example, since the names of many countries and cities mentioned in Acts no longer appear on modern maps, a Bible atlas (or a Bible that contains maps showing political divisions at the time the Bible was written) can help us realize that Paul traveled in countries that we know today as Turkey and Greece. (See Map 4).

A map of the eastern Mediterranean at the time of the Exodus shows us that the Israelites did not take the normal direct route from Egypt to Canaan, which indeed was fairly heavily traveled (see Map 1). Exodus 13:17 gives the reason: they would have had to pass through the land of the Philistines, a powerful and hostile tribe. The usual route would also have enabled Pharaoh's army to follow them more easily. So God diverted them to the wilderness of the Arabian desert, where, without interference, he could train them to be a nation.

Atlases offer other information as well. They discuss the climate, the physical characteristics of the land, effect of world events, and other matters that can help us understand the life and experience of God's people. Most atlases, for example, will point out that the land of Canaan was located in what was called the "fertile crescent," a rich agricultural area in the midst of the desert land surrounding it. So Canaan was truly a Promised Land to look forward to. At the same time, this area was coveted by many nations, so the Israelites had to fight countless territorial wars.

For specific titles and publication information of suggested resources, see "For Further Reading."

For Further Reading

Some of these books are out of print but might be obtainable in libraries and used-book stores or available in other editions than those cited.

BIBLES

Good News Bible: The Bible in Today's English Version
The New International Version
The New Revised Standard Version
The New Testament in Modern English (Phillips' translation)
The Revised New English Bible

STUDY BIBLES WITH HELPS

The Harper Study Bible. New York: Harper & Row, 1964 (RSV).
The New Jerusalem Bible. Garden City: Doubleday, 1985.
The New Oxford Annotated Bible. New Revised Standard Version. New York: Oxford University Press, 1991.
The Oxford Annotated Bible. Revised Standard Version. New York: Oxford University Press, 1962.
Serendipity Bible for Groups. Littleton, CO.: Serendipity House, 1988 (NIV).

Tools for Study

ATLASES

Aharoni, Yohanan, and Michael Avi-Yonah. *The Macmillan Bible Atlas*. New York: Macmillan, 1977.

Baly, Denis. *Basic Biblical Geography*. Minneapolis: Fortress Press, 1987.

Frank, Harry Thomas. *Discovering the Biblical World*. Maplewood, N.J.: Hammond, 1988.

Pritchard, James B. *The Harper Atlas of the Bible*. New York: Harper & Row, 1987.

Wright, George Ernest, and Floyd Vivian Filson. *The Westminster Historical Atlas to the Bible*. Philadelphia: Westminster, 1956.

CONCORDANCES

Ellison, John W. *Nelson's Complete Concordance of the RSV Bible*, 2nd ed., New York: Thomas Nelson, 1972.

Goodrick, Edward W., and John R. Kohlenberger III. *The NIV Complete Concordance*. Grand Rapids: Zondervan, 1981.

Joy, Charles R. *Harper's Topical Concordance of the Bible*, revised. San Francisco: Harper & Row, 1962.

Metzger, Bruce M., and Isobel M. *The Oxford Concise Concordance*. New York: Oxford University Press, 1962.

The RSV Handy Concordance. Zondervan, 1962.

DICTIONARIES

Achtemeier, Paul J. *Harper's Bible Dictionary*. San Francisco: Harper & Row, 1985.

Buttrick, George A., and Keith R. Crim. *The Interpreter's Dictionary of the Bible* (5 volumes). Nashville: Abingdon, 1976.

Gehman, Henry S. *New Westminster Dictionary of the Bible*. Philadelphia: Westminster, 1970.

Commentaries

SERIES

The Augsburg Commentary on the New Testament (15 volumes). Minneapolis: Augsburg, 1980–90.

The Layman's Bible Commentary (25 volumes). Atlanta: John Knox, 1959–64.

SINGLE VOLUME

Black, Matthew, and H. H. Rowley. *Peake's Commentary on the Bible*. New York: Thomas Nelson & Sons, 1962.

Brown, Raymond E., et al. *The Jerome Biblical Commentary*. Englewood Cliffs: Prentice-Hall, 1968.

Guthrie, D., and J. Motyer. *The New Bible Commentary*, revised. Grand Rapids: Wm. B. Eerdmans, 1970.

Laymon, Charles M. *The Interpreter's One-Volume Commentary on the Bible*. Nashville: Abingdon, 1971.

Mays, James L. *Harper's Bible Commentary*. San Francisco: Harper & Row, 1988.

Other Helps and Resources

Adler, Mortimer Jerome. *How to Read a Book*. New York: Simon & Schuster, 1972.

Fee, Gordon D. *New Testament Exegesis*. Philadelphia: Westminster, 1983.

Jacobson, Diane L. and Robert Kysar. *A Beginner's Guide to the Books of the Bible*. Minneapolis: Augsburg, 1991.

Koester, Craig R. *A Beginner's Guide to Reading the Bible*. Minneapolis: Augsburg, 1991.

Kuist, Howard Tillman. *These Words upon Thy Heart*. Richmond: John Knox, 1947. Out of print.

Stavey, W. David. *Groundwork of Biblical Studies*. Minneapolis: Augsburg, 1979.

Stuart, Douglas. *Old Testament Exegesis*. Philadelphia: Westminster, 1980.

Wald, Oletta. *The Joy of Discovery in Bible Study*, revised. Minneapolis: Augsburg, 1975.

Maps

MAP 1

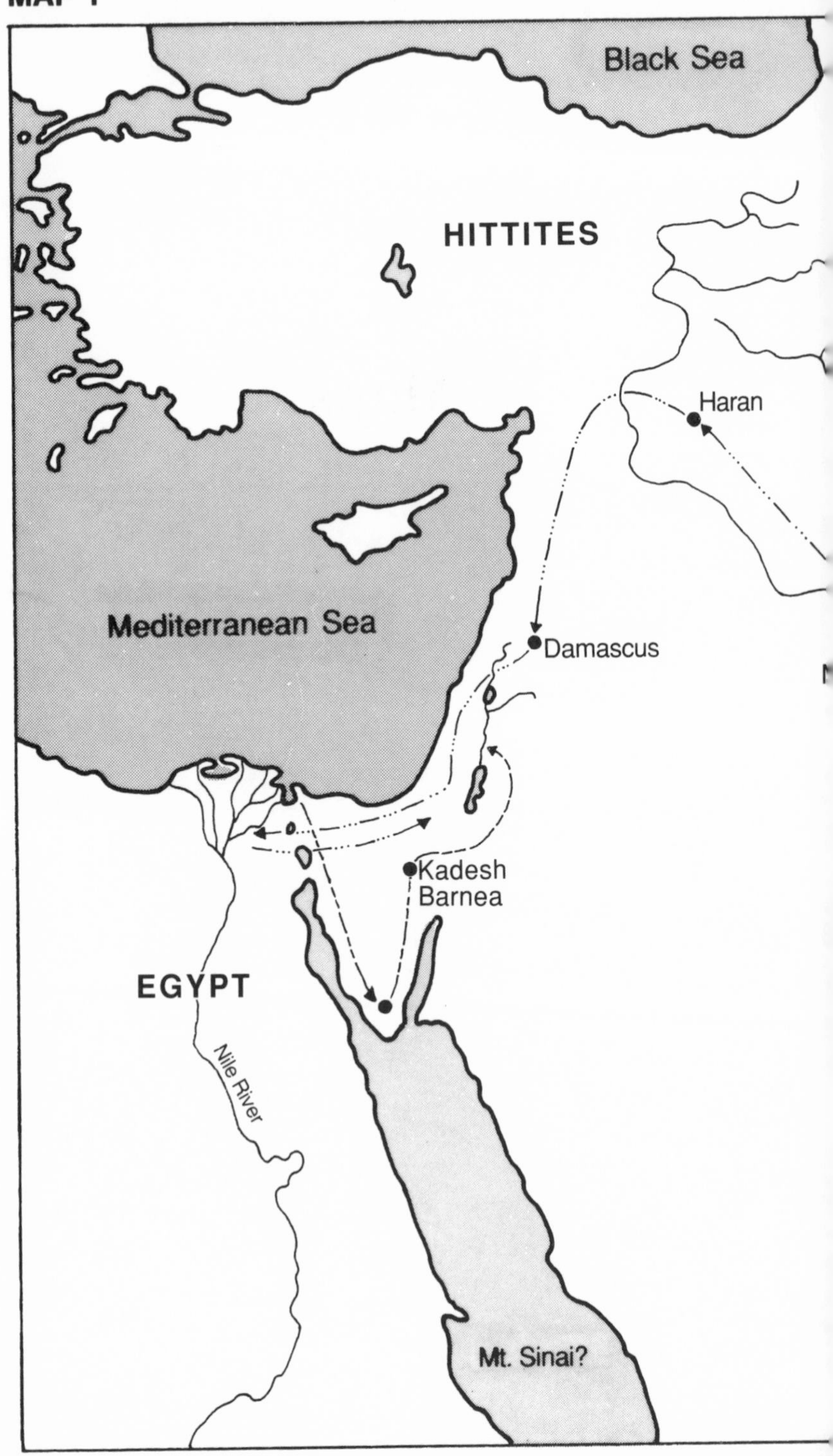

Black Sea
HITTITES
Haran
Mediterranean Sea
Damascus
Kadesh
Barnea
EGYPT
Nile River
Mt. Sinai?

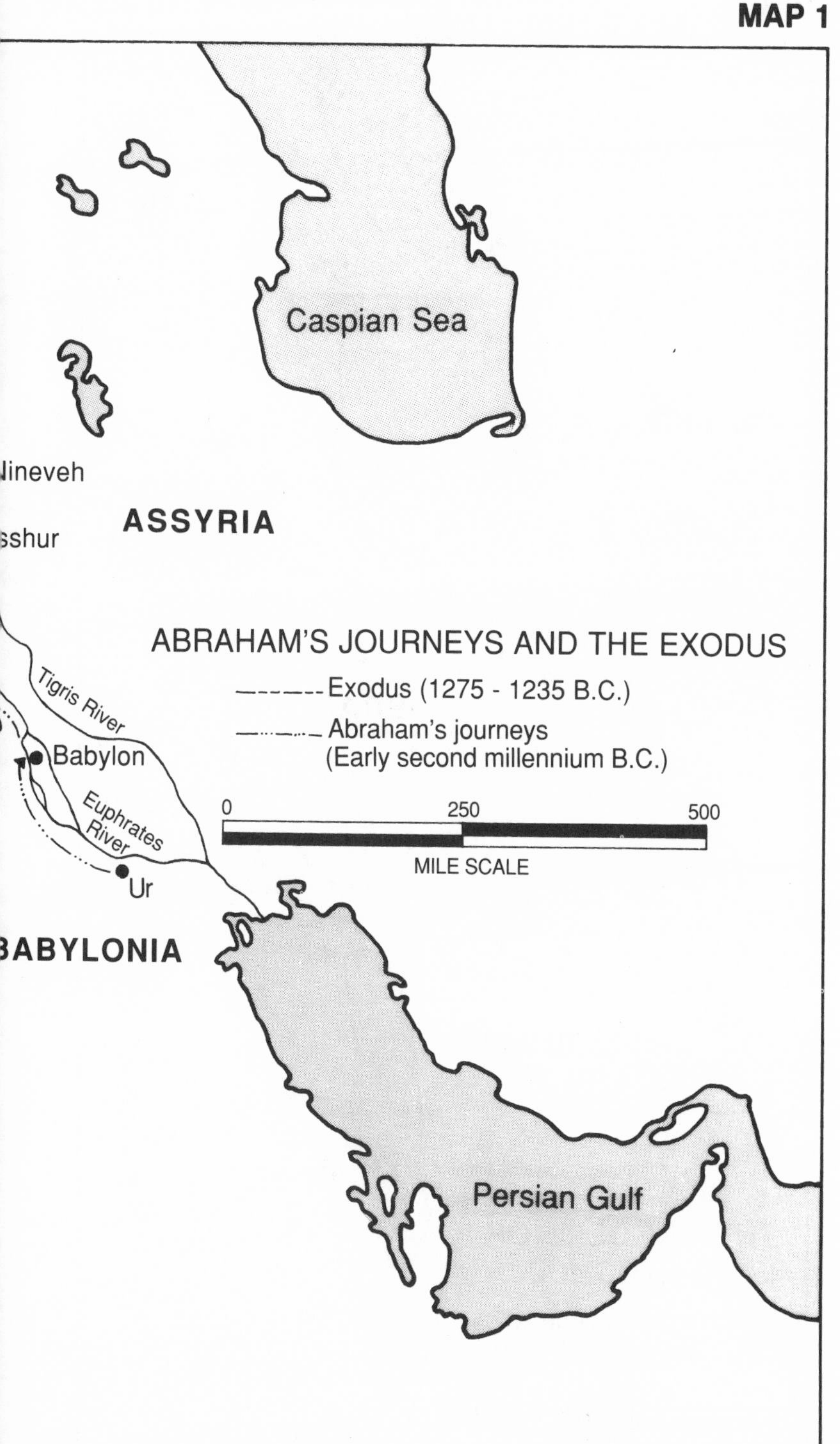
Caspian Sea
Jineveh
ASSYRIA
sshur
ABRAHAM'S JOURNEYS AND THE EXODUS
Exodus (1275 - 1235 B.C.)
Abraham's journeys
(Early second millennium B.C.)
0
250
500
MILE SCALE
Tigris River
Babylon
Euphrates River
Ur
BABYLONIA
Persian Gulf

MAP 2

Sidon
PHOENICIA
Damascus
ARAM
Tyre
The Great Sea
Samaria
ISRAEL
AMMON
Rabbah
PHILISTIA
Jerusalem
JUDAH
Gaza
MOAB
Kir-hareseth
THE KINGDOMS OF
ISRAEL AND JUDAH
Approximate boundaries
of Israel and Judah
0
25
50
MILE SCALE
EDOM

MAP 3

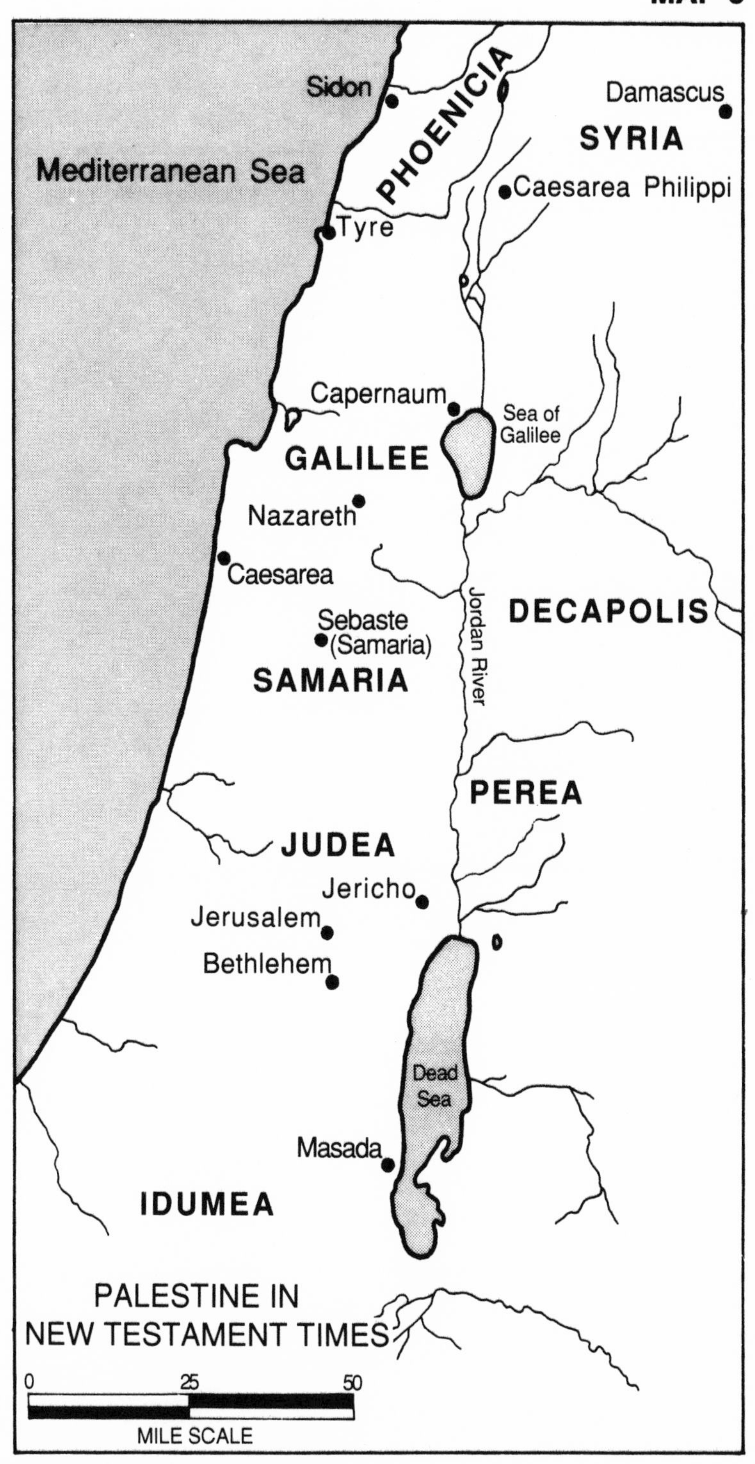

PALESTINE IN
NEW TESTAMENT TIMES

MAP 4

Rome
ITALIA
SICILIA
MALTA
MACEDONIA
Thessalonica
Berea
ACHAIA
Corinth
Mediterranean Sea
CYRENE
THE BACKGROUND OF THE NEW TESTAMENT
Places to which Paul's letters were addressed
0
250
500
MILE SCALE

MAP 4

Black Sea
roas (Alexandria)
GALATIA
ASIA
Ephesus
Colossae
Tarsus
Antioch
CYPRUS
SYRIA
Damascus
Mediterranean Sea
Caesarea
Jerusalem
ARABIA
EGYPT
Red Sea